Columbia River Gorge History
Volume One

THIRD PRINTING

TAHLKIE BOOKS
Box 355, Skamania Rt.
Stevenson, Washington 98648

INTRODUCTION

Hi-Yu Skookum Chuck

Indian Chinook Jargon words for the Great Falls on the Columbia River.

The Great River of the West was one of the last great water ways to be discovered in America. As it ran through the Cascade mountains it was squeezed into a narrow channel with a fall of thirty seven feet within a few miles. The swift water flowed over and around mammoth boulders with great turbulence and disorder and the roar of this Mighty Strong Water could be heard miles away.

The Rapids or Cascades, both names were used, caused a barrier to all boat travel, the boats and their cargo had to be portaged around these cascades. The Indians used light

3

canoes which they carried over the portage trail, but the first white men used larger boats to transport their much heavier supplies so found it much more difficult to get their equipment around the cascades.

Some of the early pioneers stayed here where they were needed, not because of generosity, but because it provided work with money to be made. Settlements grew at the portages and transportation over them improved. Steamboats came below and above the cascades so a crude railroad was built around the swiftwater.

This is some of the history of the early days in this area. The Indians were here many, many moons before the white people came, but they left no written history. This writer did not come with the first explorers so must depend on some of the history left by them, however he was a descendant of some of the early settlers and friends of others, who have given him stories which he wishes to pass on.

Yakima Indians came to the area in 1856 and attacked the portage settlement, killing and burning until the soldiers arrived. The guilty warriors escaping and the friendlys captured and some were hung.

More settlers arrived, transportation improved, Washington becomes a territory and finally county governments with taxes and road building, and a census taken in 1860.

Railroads replaced the steamboats and a power dam buries the Hi-Yu Skookum Chuck under backwater and its roar is quieted forever.

Columbus discovered America in 1492, but it remained 300 years before Gray discovered the Columbia River. Many nations were exploring the Pacific Coast during these years; many were looking for inland waterways and passed within hailing distance, without knowing the great river existed. In 1792 Captain Gray in command of the "Columbia", an American ship, made the discovery which greatly helped to save the northwest for the United States.

After Balboa's discovery of the Panama Isthmus and the Pacific Ocean in 1513, the Spanish conquerors were soon building ships in the Pacific at Panama. These first ships cruised as far north as California; but in 1542, Juan Rodriquez had sailed the western coast as far north as San Francisco Bay. His pilot, Bartolome Ferrelo, who succeeded him in command of his ship, sailed as far north as 44 degrees. The Spanish fleet now sailed further north, trading with the Indians as far north as Alaska; but on all their trips along the coast they never sighted the Great River of the West.

The famous privateer, Francis Drake, roved the Pacific Ocean, starting in 1573. His ship the "Golden Hind" preyed upon the Spanish preserves. One after another of the Spanish ports were entered and stripped of their gold and silver, and ship after ship fell into his hands. He would cut off their masts and destroy their sails so that they could not reorganize and follow him. The "Golden Hind" became so loaded with loot that to make room for gold and silver, the less valuable cargo like silk was thrown overboard. His ship became so loaded and heavy in the water that he dared not attempt a southern trip home as the Spanish warships were already searching for him and could outrun his heavily loaded ship. He hoped to discover a

5

northwest passage which many believed existed, and in looking for it he claimed the northwest coast for England; he named this territory the NEW ALBION, which showed on maps for many years.

In 1775 the topsail schooner "Sonora" (Spanish) under Juan Francisco Bodega y Quadra cruised as close to shore as possible but never sighted the Columbia River.

The vessel was so small and carried 22 men and remained at sea for eight months. It measured about 40 feet in length with a beam of only 12-1/2 feet and a depth of 8 feet. The scant depth of the hold did not permit another posture than that of being seated and the small size of the deck did not permit walking; yet these hardy men with the greatest of courage faced these hardships.

Had they sighted the mouth of the Columbia, they could have entered with their shallow draft vessel, as well as our small fishing vessels do today. They did find the Quinault River further up the Washington coast where they attempted to take on fresh water but were attacked by the Indians and lost some of their crew and water containers.

Bruno Heceta commanding the little "Santiago" almost discovered the Columbia. He sounded the depth of water at the mouth of the Columbia and detected a strong current which ran opposite the incoming tide, but because of a small crew he decided against investigating, but entered in his log that there was an entrance here to a river or an inland sea.

The British government offered a reward of 20,000 pounds in Sterling to any captain finding an inland passage from the northwest waters into Hudson Bay. In July of 1776, Captain Cook set sail, in command of two ships, the "Resolution" and the "Discovery". On their arrival along the northwest coast a storm battered his ships until it was necessary for him to return southward. In March 1778, he again sailed along the coast of Oregon and Washington; he kept the shore line in view and he named Cape Foulweather. He missed the mouth of the Columbia and wrote in his log, that no river existed.

In 1786 and 1791 two French ships explored along the Washington and Oregon coasts.

6

In 1783 the Russians sent ships under Baranoff exploring Alaska and the northwest coast.

Word was received by the Spanish that two American ships, the "Lady Washington" and the "Columbia Redivivus" had left Boston for an inspection of the northwest coast. The Spanish government then sent Martinez north to build a fort at Nootka and to hold the territory for the Spanish king, but when he arrived he found no Russians there but he found two American vessels there, the "Lady Washington" and the "Columbia", in command of Captains Kendrick and Robert Gray. The Spanish commander did not attempt to arrest the vessels but he took precaution to notify the Americans, in the name of the king, that they were not to return by these seas and coasts without securing a passport from the Spanish monarch.

Martinez arrested the "Nubiana" under command of an Englishman, Captain Douglas, and he seized the ship. Later two more English ships, the "Princess Royal" and the "Argonaut", sailed into Nootka and were seized by the Spanish commander.

The two American ships while small, were well armed with swivel guns, a few cannon, muskets, pistols, boarding pikes and cutlasses. The two captains remained friendly with Martinez who furnished them with a few supplies.

The English government at this time had no desire to have war with Spain. However, after a demand was made by the British subjects and the government could no longer submit to this pressure, England appealed to Holland and Prussia who both promised to aid England. The fleets of these nations were made ready. All British colonies were ordered to prepare, especially Canada, who was requested to cultivate friendly relations with the United States. The Spanish colonies in Central and South America were encouraged to help and get out from under the Spanish yoke. The Government of the United States decided to remain neutral.

Spain hoped to receive help from France, but at this time France was in a revolution and could not assist Spain. The Spanish had to bow to a treaty with Britain. This was fortunate for the young United States because had Britain established her title to the Oregon and Washington territory by force of arms she would not have been so likely to relinquish any of it to the American settlers later.

By 1792 no less than 7 American vessels were fur trading along the northwest coast, and the active seamen were already making discoveries which aroused the anxiety of the British. In 1801 there were 15 American vessels plying the coast.

Captain Vancouver was sent to survey the shore of the American continent on the Pacific, from latitude 30 degrees to 60 degrees. In his instructions: "It is of great importance to find any inlets of the sea, or large rivers."

Vancouver's ships were the "Discovery", of 400 tons burden, and the "Chatham", of 135 tons, in command of Lieut. W.R. Broughton. April 24th, 1792, the ships cruised along the coast of Oregon taking notes of the shore lines. The 27th they reached the mouth of the Columbia, and the Columbia bar was actually seen, and bypassed as being of no importance. Vancouver's reference to the entrance to the mighty Columbia, "not worthy of more attention." They cruised north along the Washington coast gazing at the fertile lands, not even discovering Gray's Harbor.

Early in the morning of April 29th, a sail was observed, and as they approached a friendly salute was fired by the strange boat, which was answered by the "Discovery". The strange ship was the "Columbia" from Boston under Captain Gray and flying the Stars and Stripes.

The two captains exchanged information on the colored waters at the mouth of the Columbia. Gray said that he had laid 9 days off the mouth of the great river but was unable to investigate the channel because of bad weather but that he intended to go back and try again.

Sailing down the Washington coast, Gray sighted an opening which he entered without trouble; he had discovered Gray's Harbor. It is said that Captain Gray had only one eye; but that eye must have been a very good eye, because he sighted inlets that other captains had passed by for 200 years. Gray lingered here a few days, and with improving weather, again headed south. Proceeding down the coast during the night, when dawn arrived he was off the entrance of the great river. Gray's courage and seamanship with soundings made, he entered the breakers running over the bar, he found the passageway through, and the ship "Columbia" was soon riding gently within the entrance of a new-found, great river, the River of the West. Captain Gray's log later read: "When we were over the bar we found this to be a large river of fresh water up which we steered. Many canoes came alongside."

Taken from the journal of a young officer, John Boit who was then only 17 years of age:

"The river extended to the NE. as far as the eye cou'd reach, and water fit to drink as far as the Bars, at the entrance. We directed our course up this noble River in search of a village. The beach was lin'd with natives, who ran along the shore following the ship. Soon after, 20 canoes came out, and brought a good lot of furs and salmon, which they sold us, salmon two for a board nail. The furs likewise for Copper and Cloth. They appear to view the ship with great astonishment and no doubt we were the first civilized people they had ever seen."

Gray attempted to sail up the river but the ship "Columbia" drew too much water so he turned back and anchored about where Fort Columbia was built later.

The "Columbia" was 83 feet long and 212 tons burden and required 15 feet of water to float in. Had some of the Spanish ships discovered the river, most of them could

9

have sailed right up the river. One of Heceta's ships only measured 27 feet in length and with its shallow draft, could have sailed up to the foot of the Cascades.

(The ship "Columbia" was small compared to the steamboat the "Wide West", built in Portland in 1877, which ran from Portland to the Cascades for 7 years.

"Wide West" 1,200 tons — 236 feet long

Ship "Columbia" 212 tons — 83 feet long

The "Columbia" was a sailing ship and designed with a deep draft center board so as to be able to tack broadside to the wind. The "Wide West" was a steam powered paddle wheeler so need not depend on the winds, so drew far less draft.)

Gray named this river the Columbia after his ship. May 20th, 1792 they hoisted anchor and left the river.

Five months later when Gray visited Nootka he gave Captain Vancouver the details of his discovery of Grays Harbor and the Columbia River which he had named. Vancouver soon decided to visit these new discoveries. He began his voyage down the coast with his ship the "Discovery", accompanied by the "Chatham" in command of Lieutenant Broughton. The "Discovery" and the "Chatham" arrived at the mouth of the Columbia River Oct. 19th, 1792. The "Chatham" being the smaller of the two vessels, made the entrance over the bar while the "Discovery" sailed on south. Broughton was surprised to find a small fur trading vessel, the "Jenny", of England, commanded by Captain Baker already anchored in the river.

Broughton had a ship's deck boat set in the river and with a crew of oarsmen, explored the river for a distance of 100 miles to about where Troutdale is now located. Broughton named Mt. Hood in honor of a noble Englishman; he also gave the name Point Vancouver to a point on the north side of the river.

As soon as other captains learned of Gray's discovery, many ships entered the river to trade with the Indians. Also, fresh water will kill the barnacles that attach themselves to the hulls of ships in salt water, so the captains were always ready whenever possible to lay in fresh water for a short time.

The Great River of the West was discovered by the white man, although Indians had lived on it for thousands of years. Nothing was known of the river east of Broughton's 100-mile exploration above its mouth, except, the Indians had informed him that a great falls or cascades hampered boat travel a short distance up the river from where he turned back; no white man had yet seen the river above the point where Broughton turned back down the river to his ship.

Indians' Travel Limited

Small tribes did not travel far because of the danger of larger tribes, taking slaves and killing those who resisted. Larger tribes, like the Snakes with a thousand warriors, sometimes made long voyages, even over the Rocky Mountains to hunt buffalo, but they were great horsemen. The lower Columbia River Indians were canoe travelers so they remained near their river.

No one knows the actual facts....but either a river Indian traveled east or an eastern Indian traveled west to the river and returned with the story: "A great river flows from the Rocky Mountains, west, into a great lake that isn't fit to drink (Pacific Ocean), and this great river is called the Ouragon by the Indians." This story reached as far east as the Great Lakes where Major Rogers made use of it. He submitted to King George a proposal that he take 200 men and make an overland search for this great river. In 1767 an expedition was organized under Capt. James Tute to find the head of the river and follow it to the Pacific Ocean. The first winter was spent at St. Anthony Falls with plans to leave in the spring with Sioux Indian guides. The party reached St. Anthony Falls, but because of lack of supplies the party returned and the expedition was given up.

In the articles written at that time the spelling was often different, Ouragon, Ourigan, Origan and Oregon. Ouragon is an Indian word meaning Sage Brush; the word may have come with the Spanish when they explored overland in the southwest and the Indians picked up the word. The Great River of the West runs through much sage brush country so the name could apply very well.

11

Thomas Jefferson, Third President of the U.S.

Jefferson was never able to travel to the Pacific Northwest; yet his intense interest in the Columbia River country resulted in it becoming part of the United States. He selected his secretary, Meriwether Lewis, to be the captain of an expedition to this unexplored territory. Lewis promptly named Clark, famed Indian fighter, as his co-captain.

Most everyone has read some of the fine stories of their great trip across the country and down the Columbia in 1805, and their return in 1806, so we will only mention about their travels around the Cascades in this story.

Lewis and Clark Journals

"Oct. 30. After a light breakfast on venison, Captain Lewis and five men went to the village and found the people very friendly. We got some nuts and berries, but could get no information as to the traders who visit them. It rained all day. One of the hunters killed a deer. We named the stream the "Cruzatte" (Wind River) after Peter Cruzatte who killed the deer."

This must have been a very light breakfast for these men; as their journals state, they would eat 4 deer and an elk in 24 hours, or an antelope and a buffalo in one day. These 35 young men, mostly in their 20's, living in the open, working hard from daylight until dark, were hardy eaters.

"Oct. 31. Captain Clark, Joseph Fields and Cruzatte went down the river to view the Cascades. Cruzatte was sent back to examine the rapids near shore, while Capt. Clark and Joseph Fields continued on for ten miles, after which the current became uniform. They had reached tide water. They passed a large burial place which contained many bones, sea shells, brass kettles and wooden carved images. These things we do not touch. Joseph Fields killed a sandhill crane, then the party all returned to camp. During this time, Capt. Lewis and his party unloaded the canoes and took them down, one at a time, over high rocks. We got only two over as it was hard work."

"Nov. 1. We set all hands packing the baggage over the portage—940 yards of bad rocks and slippery hillsides.

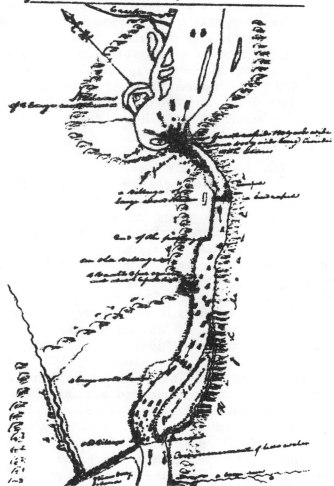

LEWIS AND CLARK MAP OF THE CASCADES, SHOWING VILLAGES

Some of the canoes were injured and had to be repaired. We brought down two other large canoes and a small one. Towards evening we had all safe below the rapids, and then camped."

That evening some Indians came to their camp and Lewis asked them about traders coming up the river. They told him Swepeton, a white man, had come up to the Cascades. Swepeton was a captain from a trading ship and may have come up the river looking for furs.

"Nov. 2. We took the baggage over the portage of a mile and a half around the lower rapids. The canoes ran this rapids without much damage. We took breakfast and made a meridian altitude, and set out. Labiche killed fourteen geese and a brant. John Collins killed one, and the Field brothers got three.

"Nov. 3. We had a heavy fog this morning which detained us until 10 A.M. Before we set out, Collins killed a large buck and Labiche killed three geese flying in the air. The Captains explored the mouth of Seal (Washougal) River. The Indians tell us it is two sleeps to the ocean."

The Lewis and Clark party remained 5 months near the mouth of the Columbia. They built winter quarters while there and lived on wild game. They had hoped to meet an American schooner while there, but no ships of any kind came into the river during this five months while they were there. They prepared to leave on their return trip up the river and over the Rocky Mountains, across the prairies and down the Mississippi River to their starting place in 1804.

"April 8, 1806. The wind blew so hard that we had to unload our canoes. Being obliged to remain here all day, we sent out Drouillard, Shannon, Collins, and Colter to hunt. Capt. Lewis walked down the river to botanize. Shields cut out Capt. Clarke's rifle and brought her to shoot very well. Our party owes much to the ingenuity of this man, by whom our guns are repaired when they get out of order, which is very often. About 1 P.M., Collins, Shannon and Colter returned, and soon afterwards Drouillard came in— all with little success. The violent waves split one of our canoes before we could get her out of the water. Late at night the sentinel detected an old Indian trying to creep into our camp to steal. He was one of six who lay encamped a couple of hundred yards below us. They all departed after our sentinel had discovered and alarmed them.

"April 9. We reloaded our canoes and set out at 7 A.M., and proceeded to pick up the Fields brothers. They had not killed any game. We did not stop, but continued to the village located on the north side about a mile below Beacon Rock. Here we halted and took breakfast. John Colter observed the tomahawk in one of the lodges which had been stolen from Capt. Clark on the 4th of November last. The natives attempted to wrest the tomahawk from Colter, but he retained it and retook our property. They denied stealing it, etc. With some difficulty we obtained five dogs and a few wappato. At 2 P.M. we set out and arrived at the first rapid. We found a good harbor and encamped. We saw deer sign, so sent Collins to hunt in the morning while the canoes were being towed above the rapids. Gibson's crew were directed to delay Collins and to collect rosen from the pine trees near our camp."

(The recovered tomahawk was one that had been traded to Indians near Washougal by ship Captain Swepeton; Captain Clark had received this tomahawk from these Indians.)

"April 10. We drew up our canoes by cords which was soon accomplished. Collins and Gibson not yet having come over, we directed Sgt. Pryor to remain with the cord to assist them in bringing their canoe up the rapid. Above, the current is so strong that it required five oars to make progress. We breakfasted at a village. Here they had a sheep-skin. The head and horns had been formed into a cap which was worn as a highly prized ornament. We obtained the cap for a knife, and two elk skins for the sheep skin. At 10 A.M. we were joined by Sgt. Pryor, Gibson and Collins who had brought up their canoe and had killed three deer. We set out and continued on the north side of the river.

"As we had only one tow-rope, we could only take one canoe at a time. By evening we arrived at the portage where we landed, and conveyed our baggage to the top of a hill where we formed a camp. We had our canoes drawn ashore and secured. One small one got loose from Drouillard and the Fields brothers. The Indians in the lower

15

village brought her up this evening, for which honesty we gave them a couple of knives.

"April 11. It rained all night, and our tents and skins which covered the men were wet. Our portage around the Cascades is 2800 yards long on a narrow slippery road. The duty of getting the canoes above the rapids was delegated to Capt. Clark, who took all but Bratton, who is so weak as to be able to walk, and three others lamed by various accidents, and one other to cook for the party. A few men were absolutely necessary to guard our baggage from the thieving Indians who crowded our camp in considerable numbers. These people are the greatest scoundrels we have met with. One had the insolence to cast stone at our men as they were walking on the portage road.

"By evening, Capt. Clark took four of the canoes above the rapids. They were much damaged by being driven against the rocks despite every precaution we took. The river appears to be some twenty-five feet higher than when we descended it last fall. On the return of our party in the evening from the head of the rapids, our men met several natives on the road. John Shields who has delayed to purchase a dog and was some distance behind, was accosted by two Indians who attempted to take the dog from him and pushed him out of the road. Shields, having no other weapon, pulled his knife, and the Indians fled through the woods. These Indians stole Scannon, Capt. Lewis's dog. Three men were sent in pursuit of the thieves, discovered the party, who left the dog and fled. They also stole an axe, but John Thompson detected the act and wrested it from them. We informed them by signs that if they made any further attempts, or insulted our men, that they would be put to death. We are concerned for future travelers; no other consideration but our numbers protected us. We kept on constant guard, and our men are disposed to kill a few of them. This evening we sent Drouillard and the Fields brothers a few miles up the river to the entrance of Cruzzatte's River (Wind River) to hunt until our arrival.

"April 12. Though it rained all of last night and this morning, we determined to haul the remaining canoe beyond the rapids. At one place the current sets with great velocity against a projecting rock, and in hauling the canoe around

16

this point the current turned her side to the stream, and despite the utmost exertions, we were compelled to loose the cord, so both canoe and cord went adrift into the stream. After breakfast all hands were employed in taking the baggage over the portage. The men who had short rifles carried them to protect our baggage from robbery or injury. Sgt. Pryor and some other men were employed the greater part of the day in repairing and calking the canoes. We remained all night at the upper end of the portage."

"April 13. The loss of one of our canoes rendered it necessary to distribute her crew and cargo among the remaining canoes. This being done, we set out at 8 A.M. We found the additional loading made our vessels hard to manage and unsafe in the event of high winds. Capt. Lewis with Sgt. Pryor and Gibson went in two small canoes, to a friendly village where they were able to purchase two additional canoes, four paddles and three dogs. He gave them two buffalo robes, four elk skins and some deer skins in exchange. His party crossed to the south side where later he found Capt. Clark's party with the large canoes. They reported they had seen nothing of Drouillard and the Fields brothers who had been sent ahead to hunt. We directed Sgt. Ordway to take the canoes just purchased, for his mess and the loading which we had carried in the lost canoe, and to have these canoes dried and pitched with rosen. We sent Sgt. Pryor back up Cruzzatte's (Wind) River in search of the hunters with two men and an empty canoe to bring back any meat they may have killed. John Shields returned after 6 P.M. with two deer. Colter had been hunting with Shields."

"April 14. This morning we were joined by Sgt. Pryor, his two men and three hunters—Drouillard, Reuben and Joseph Fields. They brought four deer which Drouillard had killed yesterday. After breakfast we departed and kept going along the north shore all day. At noon we halted at a village where we purchased five dogs, some roots, filberts and dried berries. Our men prefer fat dog meat to lean venison. After nooning, Capt. Clark and Charbonneau walked ashore, and rejoined the party some six miles upstream. We camped on a small run (near present White Salmon, Washington)."

Winship Brothers 1810

Two American brothers owned the ship "Albatross" with one of the brothers its captain, Captain Nathan Winship; fitted out and sailed into the mouth of the Columbia in May, 1810, having crossed the bar safely it sailed up the river a few miles and anchored off the south bank at what appeared beautiful, level, fertile land. They unloaded livestock and seeds and began to build a settlement. They were soon flooded by the June freshet when the river rose 20 feet or more from the melting snows. A somewhat higher site was then chosen and the houses moved.

The Indians, who had at first appeared friendly, began to show hostility. Captain Winship invited the chiefs of the natives aboard the ship for a conference. The chiefs soon expressed that they did not wish the Americans to remain. The brothers realized that with unfriendly Indians that it would be impossible to carry on trade with them; so it was a disappointed party that reloaded the ship and left.

Fort Astoria 1811

John Jacob Astor, a wealthy New Yorker, found himself as the head of the fur trade in the South. He also found that the powerful Northwest Fur Company was penetrating into his territory. He decided to expand but found the Mackinaw Fur Traders somewhat in his way, so he bought out the company and took over their territory.

Then he wanted west of the Rocky Mountains. Towards the accomplishment of this plan, Mr. Astor set about opening a branch of his large fur company on the Pacific Coast. This new branch would be called the Pacific Fur Co. and its head-quarters at the mouth of the Columbia River.

April 1811, Astor's ship, the "Tonquin", arrived with supplies and men and soon had built Fort Astoria.

Captain Thorn of the "Tonquin" was an unreasonable, ill-tempered captain and lost eight of his crew members coming over the bar and almost lost the ship. A few months later in a harbor on west Vancouver Island, after Thorn's ill-tempered treatment of the Indian visitors to the "Tonquin", the Indians murdered all on board.

David Thompson first went up the Saskatchewan in 1787 at 17 years of age. Ten years with the Hudson's Bay Co., he resigned and joined the Canadian Northwest Co. 1797. He knew the Indians as well as anyone living; he had lived with the Crees, Chipewyans, Piegans, Mandan and Kootenay nations.

His new employer ordered him to travel down the Columbia River from headwaters to its mouth and beat the Astor Party there in 1810. In coming down the river he left British flags at all the Indian villages.

This history book is only covering the Middle Columbia so only a little will be taken from Thompson's journey as he traveled between The Dalles and Cape Horn.

From David Thompson's Narrative

"We embarked and proceeded thirty miles down River, and passed about 80 families in small straggling Lodges; at one of which ten families we put ashore to smoke with them, but they were so terrified at our appearance. My men stayed on the beach, and I went forward a few paces unarmed, and sat down with a pipe and stem in hand; They sent forward two very old men, who lying flat on the ground in the most pitiful maner; crawling slowly, frequently lifting their heads a little imploring mercy; my Native Interpreter would not speak to them, and all the signs I could make gave them no confidence; close behind the men three women crawled upon their knees; lifting up their hands to me as if supplicating for their lives, the men were naked and the women nearly the same, the whole a wretched scene of destitution, it was too painful, they did not smoke with us, I gave to each of the men two inches of Tobacco, and left them. They appeared as if outcasts from the others; all those we have passed today appeared idle, we saw none of them employed with the Seine, when I spoke to the Interpreter to learn the state of these people, he gave no answer, and both himself and his wife did not wish to be spoken to about them.

"In the afternoon, when the River ran to the W S W a high mountain, isolated, of conical form, a mass of pure Snow appeared, which was Mt. Hood.

"Our Interpreter with his wife had left us; he said that he would have accompanied us to the sea, if he understood the language of the Natives further down river. I paid him as well as I could for his services. He was a fine, steady manly character, cheerful, often smiling but never laughing; he once remarked to me, when he saw my men laughing, it was allowed only to women.

"As a change is now taking place, I may remark in justice to the Natives we have passed, that however numerous and poor, not a single insult or aggression was attempted; everything we had was highly valuable to them, yet not a single article was stolen from us; they never offered us women, as is too much the custom of the Indians on the east side of the mountains; everything and every part of their conduct, was with decency and good order; they all appeared anxious to possess every article they saw with us, but at fair barter.

"Having proceeded sixteen miles, we saw the first Ash Trees with Willow and Aspen a most agreeable change from bare banks and monotonous plains."

(This was the stretch of river just below Lyle, Washington.)

"Continuing nine miles we saw two snow capped mountain peaks." (Mt. Hood and Mt. Adams.) "Both sides of the River have woods of Aspen, Cedar, Ash and Willow, having decended forty miles, the greatest part fine steady current, we came to a Village of Houses built of logs."

Thompson called these people 'Weeyarkeek'. Lewis and Clark had named them 'Wahclellahs'. Thompson having lived among the Indians since 1785, possibly was more proficient in Indian languages than Lewis and Clark.

Thompson camped here at what is now the Cascade Locks at the head of the Cascades, the 'Great Shoots' where Indian tradition claims the 'Bridge of the Gods' had fallen.

The Thompson party cut some fire wood and spent the night near the Indian Village. The next morning he endeavored to procure a guide for the rapids but was unable to, so they carried their canoes and supplies one mile around the steep rapid and re-embarked in very swift water; camping at eight-thirty PM nearly opposite Cape Horn.

When Thompson arrived at the mouth of the Columbia he found the Astor Fur Company already located there with four log houses. It was called Fort Astoria and was in charge of McDougall and Stuart.

The Astor people had only been here a few months, having arrived by schooner on the long voyage around South America. The Astor Pacific Fur Co. employees very politely received the British Thompson party.

The American Astor Company were laying plans to have some of their men under Mr. Stuart go up the Columbia from Fort Astoria to as far east as the Rocky Mountains and set up several trading stations from which to buy furs.

Although Mr. Thompson was with a rival British fur company he agreed to accompany the Stuart party in ascending the Cascades.

Thompson wrote, "July 28th. A fine morning; to my surprise, very early, apparently a young man, well dressed in leather, carrying a Bow and Quiver of Arrows, with his Wife, a young woman in good clothing, came to my tent door and requested me to give them protection, somewhat at a loss what answer to give, on looking at them, in the Man I recognized the Woman who three years ago was the wife of Boisverd, a Canadian and my servant; her conduct then was so loose that I had then requested him to send her away to her friends, but the Kootanaes were also displeased with her; she left them, and found her way from Tribe to Tribe to the Sea. She became a prophetess, declared her sex changed, that she was now a Man, dressed and armed herself as such, and also took a young woman to Wife, of whom she pretended to be very jealous; when with the Chinooks, as a prophetess, she predicted diseases to them, which made some of them threaten her life, and she found it necessary for her safety to endeavor to return to her own country at the head of this River."

Trip Up River

Having proceeded from Fort Astoria to the foot of the Cascades the party found four friendly Indians who were waiting for them with seven salmon as a present. The party put ashore on the south bank of the river at the foot

21

of the rapids and cooked the fish as all were very hungry. While eating the meal, the four native men addressed Mr. Thompson, saying, "When you passed going down to the sea, we were all strong in life, and on your return to us finds us strong to live, but what is this we hear, casting their eyes with a stern look on her, is it true that the white men (looking at Mr. Stuart and his men), haye brought with them the Small Pox to destroy us; and also two men of enormous size, who are on their way to us, overturning the Ground, and burning all the Villages and Lodges underneath it; is this true and we all soon to die?"

Mr. Thompson told them to not be alarmed, for the white . men who had arrived had not brought Small Pox, and the Natives were strong to live. Pointing to the skies he said, 'The Great Spirit is the only Master of the ground, and such as it was in the days of your grandfathers it is now, and will continue to remain the same for your grandsons.' At this they appeared much pleased and thanked Mr. Thompson for the good words. If the man woman had not been sitting behind some of the party the Indians would have plunged a dagger in her.

The Thompson party managed to carry their light canoes and supplies around the rapids with little difficulty but Mr. Stuart's log canoes could not be carried, they had to be dragged over the rough rocky paths around the rapids. Mr. Stuart had to hire Natives, who were collecting around, to help his men get the log canoes over the carrying places. About 10 A.M. they demanded payment; and would give no more help until paid; at least three times the number demanded that they had helped to carry the goods and drag the canoes. Mr. Stuart hesitated who to pay, but Dagger in hand they were ready to enforce their demands, and he had to distribute leaf tobacco, to ten times the value of their services.

Every native was armed with what was called the double Dagger, it is composed of two blades, each of six to eight inches in length, and about a full inch in width, each blade sharp pointed with two sharp edges; each blade was fixed in a handle of wood, in a right line of each other, the handle being between both blades, it is a most formidable weapon, and cannot without great danger be wrested from the holder.

22

Several of them took pleasure with a whet stone sharpening each edge and then to flourish their daggers close to the party's faces. One fellow several times came this way to Mr. Thompson who drew his pistol and pointed it at the natives' breast which soon discouraged him.

"There were several respectable looking natives who did not approve of this wild behaviour, and at times spoke a few words to them, which seemed to have some effect.

"The Natives appeared to afford no more help, and keep Mr. Stuart where he was at the foot of the Rapids; we both of us saw our danger and that we must go on as fast as possible to get clear of these people. We had expressed our surprise that we had come so far and should meet such hard treatment; that we came to supply their wants, and not to kill or be killed, and if they continue to threaten our lives, they must not expect to see us again; upon this they called upon the young men, to go and assist Mr. Stuart up the rapids, and over the carrying places, which they willingly and readily did; but there was a large party that rendered no assistance; we soon accended the Rapids, we put our canoe in the water and in it placed our baggage ready to set off.

"This we had done sooner than the natives expected, and we were waiting to learn how Mr. Stuart was getting forward; our place was on a level rock of basalt which formed the rim of the River, and nearly on a level with it, so that we could not be surrounded."

(This would be about where the upper end of the old steamboat locks joined the river above the rapids in 1896 at Cascade Locks.)

"As this was the last place where we could be attacked at a disadvantage in position, I was anxious to see what these people would do; our arms were in good order and each of us in his place; about fifteen yards from us, running parallel with the River, was a bank of gravel, about twenty feet in height, steep, except opposite us, where it was broken into a slope. This bank formed the edge of the flat ground, we were scarcely ready before a number of them came over the flat area to the sloping part of the bank, each armed with a double Dagger, a Bow and three Quivers of Arrows.

They formed three rows on the slope, from the top to half down the bank, the Arrows were all poisoned, as we afterwards learned; each man had one arrow to the bow, and three more in the hand that held the bow; their bringing so many Quivers of Arrows was meant to intimidate us.

"I directed my men, who formed a line three feet from each other, to direct a steady aim at the most important men, and not vary their aim. My orders were, as soon as they drew an arrow to fire on them, but not before; in this anxious posture we stood opposed to each other for fifteen minutes, shortly afterwards the top row started breaking up and in a few minutes the whole of them retired, to our great satisfaction; for a single shower of arrows would have laid us all dead; we heartily thanked God.

"Mr. Stuart soon after came, and by hard exertion we got everything he had over. We then went up River about half a mile and camped late, very thankful that we were once more together.

"On talking over the events of the day, we hardly knew what to make of these people; they appeared a mixture of kindness and treachery. They steal all they can lay their hands on, and nothing can be got from them which they have stolen.

"Very early the next morning at daylight we set off; fortunately for us the ground for upwards of five miles was inundated, two canoes with two Indians in each canoe came up and followed us, keeping close behind us, these called aloud and were answered by a party on shore, keeping on the edge of the overflowed grounds; and thus following us, and calling to each other for the five miles, at the end of this distance was a Point of Pine Woods, with dry banks, very fit for an attack as the current obliged us to keep close to the shore, so far as the water would allow us, the calling to each other became more frequent, which also plainly showed us where they were; when within three hundred yards of the Point to their disappointment, we sheered off from shore, and crossed the River, which from here is a thousand yards in width, and thus set ourselves free from these Scoundrels."

(They were then heading for what is now Home Valley.)

From Astoria to the Narrows (1811)
by Alexander Ross

"Notwithstanding the departure of the ship and our reduced numbers, measures were taken for extending the trade; and the return of Mr. Thompson up the Columbia, on his way back to Canada, was considered as affording a favorable opportunity for us to fit out a small expedition, with the view of establishing a trading post in the interior. We were to proceed together for the sake of mutual protection and safety, our party being too small to attempt anything of this kind by itself. Accordingly, Mr. David Stuart, myself, Messrs. Pillet and McLennan, three Canadian voyageurs, and two Sandwich Islanders, accompanied by Mr. Thompson's party and the two strangers, in all twenty-one persons, started from Astoria at eleven o'clock on the twenty-second of July, 1811.

"In two clumsy Chinook canoes, laden each with eighteen packages of goods of ninety pounds each, we embarked to ascend the strong and rapid Columbia; and considering the

25

unskillfulness of our party generally in management of such fickle craft, the undertaking was extremely imprudent."

"On the 24th the party camped at the mouth of the Wallamitte (Willamet) River and gave some trifling presents to a principal chief, named Kiasno. The next night they camped at Wasoughally. The 27th the party camped at the foot of a large rock they named Inshoach Castle (Beacon Rock). Mr. Thompson informed the party that they were but a short distance from the Cascades.

"After making some distance with paddles we had recourse to poles and then to the hauling line. We had no sooner stepped ashore than a great concourse of Indians assembled at a short distance from us, and after holding a consultation, came moving on in a body to meet us, or rather, as we thought to welcome our arrival. The parley being ended and the ceremony of smoking over, they pointed up the river, signifying that the road was open for us to pass. Embarking again, we pushed on, and passing the Strawberry Island (named by Lewis and Clark, now called Hamilton Island), we continued for some distance farther, and finally put on shore at the end of the portage, or carrying place, across the river on the south bank.

"Here the Indians crowded about us in fearful numbers, and some of them became very troublesome. A small present being made to each of the chiefs. They then pointed across the portage, or carrying place, as much as to say, 'All is clear; pass on.'

"From this point we examined the road over which we had to transport the goods, and found it to be 1,450 yards long, with a deep descent near the Indian villages, at the far end, with up and down hills, and side hills most of the way, besides a confusion of rocks, gullies, and thick woods from one end to end. To say that there is not a worse path under the sun would be going a step too far, but to say that for difficulty and danger few could equal it, would be saying but the truth. Certainly nothing could be more discouraging than our present situation: obstacles on every side, by land, by water, and from Indians, all hostile alike. Having landed the goods and secured the canoes, we commenced the laborious task of carrying, and by dividing ourselves in the best possible manner for safety, we managed to get all safe

26

over by sunset. Not being accustomed myself to carry, I had, of course, as well as some others, to stand sentinel; but seeing the rest almost wearied to death, I took hold of a roll of tobacco and after adjusting it on to my shoulder, and holding it fast with one hand, I moved on to ascend the first bank; at the top of which, however, I stood breathless, and could proceed no farther. In this awkward plight, I met an Indian and made signs to him to convey the tobacco across, and that I would give him all the buttons on my coat, but he shook his head and refused. Thinking the fellow did not understand me, I threw the tobacco down, and pointing to the buttons one by one, at last he consented, and off he set at a full trot and I after him; just as we had reached the camp at the other end, he pitched it down a precipice of two hundred feet in height, and left me recover it the best way I could. Off I started after my tobacco, and if I was out of breath after getting up the first bank, I was ten times more so now. During my scrambling among the rocks to recover my tobacco, not only the wag that played me the trick, but fifty others, indulged in a hearty laugh at my expense; but the best of it was, the fellow came for his payment, and wished to get not only the buttons, but the coat along with them. I was for giving him—what he richly deserved—buttons of another mould, but peace in our present situation was deemed the better policy; so the rogue got the buttons and we saw him no more.

Now Cascade Locks
   "Before leaving this noted place, the first barrier of the Columbia, we may remark that the whole length of the cascade, from one end to the other, is two and a half miles. We were now encamped at the head, or upper end, of them, where the whole river decends in high and swelling surges with great fury.
   "All the Indians we saw about this place were in small camps or villages, and might number 250 or 300. They called themselves Cathleyacheyachs, and we could scarcely purchase from the lazy rascals fish and roots enough for supper. In dress, appearance, and habits they differed but

27

little from those around Astoria, but they spoke a different language, although many of them understood and spoke Chinook also.

"At first we had formed a favorable opinion of them; but their conduct soon changed, for we had no sooner commenced transporting our goods than they tried to annoy us in every kind of way—break our canoes, pilfer our property, and even threaten ourselves, by throwing stones and pointing their arrows at us. We were not, however, in a situation to hazard a quarrel with them, unless in the utmost extremity; and it certainly was with great difficulty, and by forbearance on our part, that we got so well off as we did. After finishing the labor of the day, we arranged ourselves for the night. The Indians all assembled again about our little camp, and became very insolent and importunate; they looked at everything, and coveted all they saw. Indeed, we were afraid at one time that we would have to appeal to arms; but fortunately, after distributing a few trifling presents among the principal men, they smoked and left us, but we kept a constant watch all night. The only domestic animal we saw among them was a dog.

"On the 29th, early in the morning, we prepared to leave the Cascades; but the bank being steep and the current very strong where we had to embark, we did not venture off before broad daylight, and before that time the Indians had crowded about us as usual. Their pilfering propensities had no bounds. The more we gave them the more they expected, and of course the more trouble they gave us; and notwithstanding all our care and kindness to them, they stole our canoe-axe and a whole suit of clothes, excepting the hat, belonging to Mr. McLennan, which we were unable to recover. We had no sooner embarked, however, than Mr. McLennan, in his usual good humor, standing up in the canoe and throwing his hat amongst them, said, 'Gentlemen, there's the hat; you have got the rest; the suit is now complete,' and we pushed off and left them.

"Immediately above the cascade the river resumes its usual breadth, with a smooth and strong current. The day being exceedingly warm, we made but little headway. In the evening we passed a small river on our left, near which we encamped for the night. Here we had promised ourselves a quiet night and sound sleep, but the Indians, finding us out, partly deprived us of both, as we had to keep watch. They were but few, however, and therefore peaceable.

"On the 30th we set off early, leaving the five Indians who slept in our camp last night sitting by the fire, enjoying a pipe of tobacco. As we proceeded, the country became more bold, rough, and mountainous, but still covered with thick woods and heavy timber. The day being very hot, we encamped early on a very pleasant and thickly wooded island.

"On the 31st, after breakfast, Mr. Thompson and party left us. We remained in camp until the following day and then proceeded on toward the Long Narrows."

More of Mr. Ross's travels can be read in 'Adventures of the First Settlers on the Oregon'.

"The two strangers remained with us." Later on when the party reached Okanogan, Mr. Ross said, "In the account of our voyage I have been silent as to the two strangers who cast up at Astoria, and accompanied us from thence; but have noticed already that instead of being man and wife, as they at first gave us to understand, they were in fact both women—and bold, adventurous Amazons they were. In accompanying us, they sometimes shot ahead and at other times loitered behind, as suited their plans. The stories they gave out among the unsuspecting and credulous natives, as they passed, were well calculated to astonish as well as attract attention. Brought up, as they had been near the whites—who rove, trap, and trade in the wilderness—they were capable of practicing all the arts of well instructed cheats; and to effect their purpose the better, they showed the Indians an old letter, and told them that they had been sent by the Great White Chief, with a message to apprise the natives in general that gifts, consisting of goods and implements of all kinds, were forthwith to be poured in upon them; That the Great White Chief knew their wants, and was just about to supply them with everything their hearts could desire; that the whites had hitherto cheated the Indians, by selling goods, in place of making presents of them as directed by the Great White Chief. These stories, so agreeable to the Indian ear, were circulated far and wide, and not only received as truths, but procured so much celebrity for the two cheats that they were the objects of attraction at every village and camp on the way: nor could we, for a long time, account for the cordial reception they met with from the natives, who loaded them for their good tidings with the most valuable articles they possessed—horses, robes, leather, and Higaus; so that on our arrival at Oakinackin they had no less than twenty-six horses, many of them loaded with the fruits of their false reports."

The Astor fur traders then set up business collecting furs from the Indians and building Fort Okanogan, the chief interior post of the Pacific Fur Company. The following year they loaded their furs and started back to Astoria. On their long trip down while near Umatallow River a little after sunrise, they noticed a large group of Indians being assembled together, when they were hailed loudly in English to "come on shore." The party hesitated momentarily, when they heard the call again, so they steered toward shore, when to the surprise of all, who should be standing there but Mr. Crooks and John Day. They could hardly be recognized as white men, so let us have Mr. Crooks give us an account of their condition:

"After being left by Mr. Hunt, we remained for some time with the Snakes, who were very kind to us. When they had anything to eat we ate also; but they soon departed, and being themselves without provisions, of course they left us without any. We had to provide for ourselves the best way we could. As soon, therefore, as the Indians went off, we collected some brushwood and coarse hay and made a sort of wigwam, to shelter us from the cold. We then collected some firewood; but before we got things in order, John Day grew so weak that when he sat down he could not rise again without help. Following the example of the Indians I dug some roots for our sustenance, but not knowing how to cook them, we were nearly poisoned. In this plight we fortunately let the fire go out, and for a day and night we both lay in a torid state, unable to strike fire, or to collect dry fuel. We had now been a day without food, or even a drink of water, and death appeared inevitable. But Providence is ever kind. Two straggling Indians, happening to come our way, relieved us. They made us a fire, got us some water, and gave us something to eat; but seeing some of the roots that we had collected to eat, they gave us to understand that they were poison. If we had had a fire, those very roots would have been our first food. These poor Indians stayed with us for two days and on departing they gave us about two pounds of venison.

"On the same day, after the Indians had left us, a very large wolf came prowling about our hut, when John Day, with great exertion and good luck, shot the ferocious animal dead, and to this fortunate hit I think we owed our lives. The flesh of the wolf we cut up and dried and laid it by for some future emergency, and in the meantime feasted upon the skin; nor did we throw away the bones, but pounded them between stones, and with some roots made a kind of a broth, which to our present circumstances we found very good. After we recovered our strength a little and were able to walk, we betook ourselves to the mountains in search of game; and when unsuccessful in the chase we had recourse to dried wolf. For two months we wandered about, barely sustaining life with our utmost exertions. All this time we kept traveling until we happened, by mere chance, to fall on to the Umatallow River; and then following it we made the Columbia on the fifteenth of April. Our clothes being torn and worn out, we suffered severely from the cold; but on reaching this place, the Indians were very kind to us. This man—pointing to an old gray-headed Indian called Yeckatatpam, was very kind to us. After resting ourselves for two days with the good old man and his people, we set off, following the current in the delusive hope of being able to reach Astoria.

"We had proceeded on our journey nine days without interruption and were not far from the Falls when a considerable number of Indians collected around us in the usual friendly manner. After some little time, however, one of them got up on the pretense of measuring the length of my rifle with his bow, took it in his hands; another Indian did the same with John Day's gun. The moment the two guns were in their possession the two Indians darted out of the crowd to some distance, and assuming a menacing attitude, pointed them at us; in the same instant all the others fled

31

from us and joined the two who had taken the guns. All began to intimate to us by signs, in the most uproarious and wild manner, that some of their people had been killed by the whites.

"The Indians then closed in upon us, with guns pointed and bows drawn, on all sides, and by force stripped us of our clothes, ammunition, knives, and everything else, leaving us as naked as the day we were born, and by their gestures it appeared evident that there was a disposition on their part to kill us; but, after a long and angry debate, in which three old men seemed to befriend us, they made signs for us to be off. We took off expecting every moment to receive a ball or arrow. After traveling some distance we looked back and saw the savages quarreling about the division of the booty; this gave us time to get into the hills. All that day we traveled without tasting food and at night concealed ourselves among the rocks, without fire, food or clothing. We headed back up river and in seven days we were back with our good friend Yeckatatpam who received us again and gave us these skins to cover our nakedness, as you now see.

"The good old man then killed a horse, which his people cut up and dried for us, and with that supply we resolved to set out this very day and retrace our steps back again to St. Louis, and when you came in sight we were in the act of tying up our meat, regretting, most of all, that we had no way of recompensing our good and faithful friend Yeckatatpam."

Mr. Stuart of the fur traders then called the old man to him and clothed him from head to foot for his friendly services. The party then pushed off taking Crooks and John Day with them. On arriving at the place where the robbery occurred the party put ashore, but the Indians, having notice of their approach, fled into the hills. They again passed the Cascades and continued on to Astoria.

"Dec. 1813. On our way down the Columbia such was the mildness of the winter that not a speck of ice was to be seen. At the head of the Cascades, a place always notorious for its bad population we encamped, and were disturbed all night by the whooping and yelling of savages, who kept prowling in the woods around us. Notwithstanding the strictest watch, several arrows were shot into our camp and a man named

32

Plessis was wounded in the ear. We fired several shots into the woods from a three pounder, which kept the Indians at a distance. In the morning we passed the Cascades peaceably..

"Below the Cascades there is no impediment whatever to navigation of the river, by night or day. The brigade, therefore, went sweeping down the current in the dark. Next morning at daybreak, we met, opposite to the Wallamitte, two North West canoes and twenty men, under the direction of Messrs. Keith and Alexander Stuart, two partners of the North West Company, on their way to the interior, We breakfasted together and I strongly advised them to turn back, since so small a party could never hope to pass through the hostile tribes of the Cascades in safety. They, however, made light of the matter, giving me to understand that they were North Westers! so we parted and they proceeded. While talking on the subject of danger one of those swelling fellows, such as may be ordinarily seen stuck up in the end of a North West canoe, with a bonnet of feathers surpassing in size the head of a buffalo bull, turned round to my men and said, 'Do you think we are Americans? We will teach the Indians to respect us.' "

The early travelers along the river dreaded the Indians at the Upper Cascades more than any others in the Northwest when one goes back into rare histories like Columbia River by Alexander Ross, 1849.

On Messrs. Keith and Stuarts' arrival at the portage trail of the Cascades the Indians collected, as usual in large numbers; but did not attempt anything till the people had got involved and dispersed in the portage. They then seized the opportunity, and began to help themselves; drew bows, brandished their lances, and pounced upon the gun cases, powder kegs and bales of goods. Mr. Stuart tried to defend himself, but owing to the wet weather his gun missed fire several times, and before any assistance could reach him he had received three arrows. The Indians fled to their strongholds behind the rocks and trees. To save the property in this moment of alarm and confusion was impossible; to save themselves and carry off Mr. Stuart, was the first consideration. They, therefore, made for their canoes with all haste, and embarked. The moment they pushed off and shot down the river with all haste. Both canoes paddled day and night down river to across from the Wallamitte (now called the Willamette).

This disaster set the whole Northwest machinery at Fort George (Astoria) in motion. Revenge for the insult, and a heavy retribution on the heads of the whole Cath-le-yach-e-yach nation was decreed. Eighty-five picked men and two Chinook interpreters, under Mr. M'Tavish's command took off in ten sailboats from Ft. George (Astoria) for the cascades. Every man armed, two big guns, six swivels, cutlasses, hand-grenades, and handcuffs, with ten days provisions. They all arrived safe on the third day, and cast anchor at Strawberry Island near the foot of the rapids. (As near as I can figure from its numerous mention, this would be Hamilton Island.) The next morning on landing at the lower end of the portage the formidable armament struck such terror into the Cascade Indians that they could not be brought out of the wilderness. Next morning the two Chinook interpreters were sent ashore to summon the Indians to appear and give account of their late conduct, and they were desired, if they wished mercy to be extended towards them, to deliver up at once all the property plundered from the expedition of Messrs. Keith & Stuart.

The Cath-le-yach-eyach chiefs, not the least intimidated by the hostile array before them, sent back this answer, "The whites have killed two of our people, we will kill four of your people in return." The Indians had sent off all their women and children into the woods; then arming themselves they took up a stand behind rocks and trees. M'Tavish then sent the two interpreters to invite them to a parley, and to smoke the pipe of peace. The Indians returned the answer that, "The white man leave or be killed."

The next day the interpreters were sent to sound them again. Towards noon a few stragglers and slaves approached the camp and delivered up a small parcel of cloth torn up in pieces and scarcely worth picking up. In the evening two of the principal Indians also brought to M'Tavish a small parcel of odds and ends, little better than the last. Being interrogated on the subject of the stolen property, they denied being present at the time, and had cunning enough to make their innocence appear and also convince

M'Tavish that they were using their utmost influence to bring the Indians to terms, and deliver up the property.

During the third day, the Indians came out twice to the verge of the woods, every moment of the whites was seen by the Indians, but not a movement of the Indians behind the trees could be discerned by the whites. Next morning it was discovered that some Indians lurking about had entered the camp and carried off two guns and some other supplies, and the Indians were seen occasionally flying from place to place, and now and then whooping or yelling, as if some plan of attack were in contemplation. These circumstances made the whites reflect on their own situation. The savages, sheltered behind trees and rocks, might cut them all off without being seen, it was also intimated by the interpreters that the Indians might all this time be increasing their numbers by foreign auxiliaries. They therefore, without recovering the property, firing a gun, or securing a single prisoner, sounded retreat, and returned home on the ninth day—making the matter ten times worse than it was before. The warlike expedition was turned into ridicule by the Cath-le-yach-e-yachs, and had a worse effect on the Indians.

Ross——29 Oct. 1813, with 72 men

"On arriving at the first rapids few Indians made their appearance; and their peaceable demeanor, we did not think it necessary to observe our usual caution in guarding the portages. We passed the first unmolested, and had carried about one-third of the goods over the second, when we were alarmed by a loud cry, and immediately after one of the men appeared, and stated that he and another man had been attacked by a large party of natives, who had knocked them down, and robbed them of two bales of dry goods, with which they made off with into the woods, and he feared others of the men would be attacked.

"On arriving about the middle of the portage, where the village was situated, we found the pathway guarded by fifty or sixty Indians with their war-shirts on, and fully armed, apparently determined to dispute the passage. The moment

35

they perceived our approach they placed their arrows in their bows, which they presented at us, at the same time jumping like kangaroos backwards and forwards, and from left to right, in such a manner as to render it almost impossible to take a steady aim at any of them."

"Mr. Stuart informed the Indians that he did not wish to fight—but that if the stolen goods were not returned, the white men would destroy their village and take all their property.

"We were somewhat puzzled at their conduct; but as we were anxious to avoid bloodshed, and at the same time to recover the stolen property, Mr. Stuart judged it prudent to wait the arrival of the other party.

The Columbia River

"In a few seconds Messrs. LaRocque and M'Gillivray with their men appeared at the rear of the Indians, who were this placed between two fires; but they had the sagacity to perceive that we could not act on the offensive without endangering our own lives. About one half of them therefore quickly turned round, and by this movement presented a hostile front to each of our small parties. During this time none of their old men, women, or children, made their appearance; and as Mr. Stuart supposed they had been conveyed from the village, he requested Mr. LaRocque to advance with a few of his men into the wood on his right, and at the same time sent me with five of our party to the left, ordering each of us to seize all men, women, and children we could find, for the purpose of detaining them as hostages until the property should be returned. Messrs. Stuart and M'Gillivray, with the remainder of the men, still kept possession of the pathway in front and rear of the village, and the enemy for some time were ignorant of the ruse de guerre we had adopted. I proceeded about forty yards in an oblique direction to the left, with my party, when we imagined we heard voices before us. We therefore advanced slowly and cautiously a few paces farther, until we arrived at a large rock. I sent three men round one end of it, and proceeded myself with the remaining two round and, as we turned the left corner, we perceived three old men, with several women and children, sitting round a fire, some of whom were sharpening iron and flint heads for arrows, which, after being heated in the fire, were dipped into a wooden bowl containing a thick blackish liquid. On observing us they attempted to escape, when the other three men appeared. We instantly seized their armoury, and took two of the old men, three women, and some children prisoners. They were much frightened, and thought we would put them to death, but on our explaining that they would sustain no injury if our goods were returned, they appeared more tranquil, and came with us quietly until we reached Mr. Stuart, who was still in the same situation. LaRocque was equally fortunate, and had captured one old man, four women, and five children, on his side of the wood, with whom he had just appeared in sight as my party arrived.

"The warriors were quite staggered at finding we had made so many prisoners, and fearing we might follow their own mode, which was either to kill them or make them slaves, they at once laid down their arms, and offered to go in search of the bales, provided we would liberate the prisoners. Mr. Stuart replied that none of them would be injured, but that they should remain in custody until the property was restored and our people safely over the portage. A guard was then stationed over the prisoners, and word was sent to M'Donald to order his men to re-commence the carriage of the goods, during the progess of which we kept up a chain of sentinels en route. By the time we had nearly finished, three of the Indians, whose wives were captives, brought a great part of the contents of the bales, which they alleged they took by force from the thieves, who had cut open the envelopes and concealed the remainder; and they therefore hoped we would allow their relations to return home. Mr. Stuart told them he was determined not to allow one of them to stir until every article that had been stolen was brought back. The eldest of the three declared that it was very unjust of the white men to punish him and his relations for the dishonesty of others, and that when he expected a reward for his exertions in bringing back so much property, he found his wife and children were to be detained as slaves. All this appeared very plausible; but we recognized this very fellow as one of the most prominent and active of the armed band, and apparently their leader.

"He made some farther remonstrances to the same effect; but finding we were inflexible, he went away with his two companions, and in about half an hour after returned, accompanied by several others, with the remainder of the stolen property. They alleged the thieves had run away, and on asking them for their chief, they said he was absent. The canoes having been now laden, Mr. Stuart told them that he should release their friends and relations for this time, but that if another attempt was ever made, the white people would punish them severely, and as a mark of his anger at their late conduct, he would not then give them the usual gratuity of tobacco. The prisoners were then released, and we pushed off.

Attack at Night

"As it was rather late we could not advance more than three miles, when we encamped in a small cove on the left side, behind which was a thick wood of hazel, beech, and pine. We had a large fire at the end of the camp; and the party was divided into two watches. The forepart of the night passed off quietly; but about two o'clock in the morning we were alarmed by one of the flank sentinels being brought to the centre wounded. He stated that he and two of his comrades had approached the fire for the purpose of lighting their pipes, when several arrows were discharged at them from the wood, one of which wounded him in the left arm, upon hearing this, Messrs. LaRocque and M'Donald, who commanded the watch, fired into the wood. The tents were immediately struck, and the men ordered to withdraw from the fires and concentrate themselves behind the canoes. About ten minutes afterwards a shower of arrows was discharged from the same place, followed by loud yells; but some passed over our heads, while others were intercepted by the canoes, in which they remained fast. The two watches were now ordered to fire a volley alternately, and

38

load immediately. The first discharge caused much rustling among the leaves and branches; the second, as we supposed, completely dislodged them, and from moans heard from the retreating savages we had reason to think that some of our balls took effect. It was a cold damp morning, and what between the fatigues and dangers of the preceding day, fear, chilliness, and the want of sleep, our men did not seem much disposed for fighting. Mr. Stuart therefore ordered each man a double allowance of rum, "to make his courage cheerie," and the moment daylight began to dawn the canoes were thrown into the water, and the lading immediately commenced.

"The canoe-men embarked first; and we followed. The last man on shore was a celebrated half-breed hunter, named Pierre Michel, and just as he was about stepping into his canoe, one of the men perceived a tall Indian emerge from the wood, and bend his bow. He had scarcely time to warn Michel of his danger ere the arrow winged its flight, and completely pierced his hat, in which it remained fixed. Michel instantly turned round, and as the savage retreated into the wood, fired, and hit him somewhere about the knee. He then sprang into the canoe. We discharged a few more shots, pushed off, and paddled quickly to the opposite side. From the greyish twilight of the morning we had only an imperfect view of the Indian; but the men who had the best opportunity of seeing him were of opinion that he was the same who had expostulated the day before about the detention of his wife, after he had brought back part of the goods. We landed about ten miles farther up on the right side, on an open point; and as the canoes wanted repairing, and the men stood in need of repose, it was deemed expedient to remain there during the day. I forgot to mention that one of our Iroquois hunters sucked the wound which the man had received from the arrow in the arm: this probably saved the poor fellow's life, as we had reason to think that the arrow was poisoned. The day after, the arm became quite black from the wrist to the shoulder; but, by the use of caustic applications, the dangerous symptoms were dispersed, and in a few weeks he recovered his ordinary health.

Dog-eating

"From this place to the narrows and falls we saw no Indians; but at the latter we found about fifteen lodges of the Eneeshurs. As our provisions were nearly consumed, we were obliged to purchase twenty dogs from them. It was the first time I had eaten any of the flesh of this animal, and nothing but stern necessity could have induced me to partake of it. The president of our mess called it 'mutton', which it somewhat resembles in taste. We generally had it roasted, but the Canadians preferred it boiled, and the majority of them seemed to think it superior to horse-flesh. In this, however, I entirely differ from them, for the latter is a cleaner animal, and in taste bears a stronger resemblance to beef than the dog does to mutton. The natives behaved themselves quietly, and did not show any disposition to pilfer.

"From hence to the Wallah Wallah River we obtained no horses, and our chief support consisted of 150 dogs, which we purchased at the different villages. The Wallah Wallahs received us in their usual friendly manner, and we purchased from them about twenty good horses."

The Fur Trade and the Northwest

When the North West Company followed David Thompson's journey and developed their own trade to the Columbia they met a lively opposition from the Astorians, working inland (via the Cascades) to Okanogan, Kamloops, Spokane and the Snake River. But the War of 1812 isolated the Astorians, and in June 1813 they sold their post to the Nor'westers, thus anticipating capture by a ship which had been sent from England.

The Nor'westers created a Columbia Department bringing goods in with a transport system. They made profits, and continued to do so when in 1818 the British Government, anxious to placate the Americans, acquiesced in the return to the United States of the North West post. But the convention of Oct. 20, 1818, gave free access to citizens of the United States and of Great Britain for a period of ten years,

40

and under this system of Joint Occupation the Nor'westers were still able to trade freely.

The Americans outclassed the North West Company in marine shipping so were too strong in competition for the Nor'westers and controlled the China trade along with the East Indian Company. The British company turned toward the Snake River country, hoping to head off the furs coming down the Columbia to the American Company. In 1823, a Snake country expedition was organized, under a hardened Nor'wester, Finan MacDonald, who brought in a fair amount of furs; but MacDonald swore he never would go back in to the Snake country again. He had found the Indians of this area very unruly and by the time MacDonald got back to the North West Company headquarters at Spokane he had killed about seventy Indians and lost six of his men.

In 1824 Peter Skene Ogden was in charge of the command at Spokane. Alexander Ross returned from a fur collecting expedition with some furs, but he had met opposition from Americans led by Jedediah Smith. The Americans were confident and effective, and Ross was not the man to face them.

1825—Fort Vancouver was the first settlement in what is now the state of Washington.

1828—A party led by Jedediah Smith was massacred by the Umpqua Indians, it was to Fort Vancouver that Smith fled, and it was a Hudson's Bay party that carried out a punitive raid.

1824—Chief Factor John McLoughlin became in charge of the Columbia Department. He was a Nor'wester but coalition with the Hudson's Bay Company left him in charge.

The main depot inherited from the Nor'westers, Fort George, was, however south of the Columbia, and there was little hope of retaining it.

1825—McLoughlin moved the depot upriver 75 miles to Jolie Prairie where Fort Vancouver was then built. The move was in tune as it appeared Oregon would gradually slide into the hands of the United States.

1831-32—Nathaniel Wyeth, founder of the Oregon Colonization Society, started out with a party of thirty-one would-be settlers and brought eleven of them through to Fort Vancouver. They had to be helped on their way by the

41

Hudson's Bay Company's posts, and they suffered severely. But Wyeth came again in 1834, this time representing the Columbia River Fishing and Trading Company. He now brought twenty-four men overland, and he got a cargo of goods round by sea. He set up a supply station to supply goods to American trappers at Fort Hall. He was to take payment in furs. This didn't fit in with the British so he was driven out of business. Wyeth's episode revealed American interest in the Columbia.

1836—William Slocum visited the Columbia and made a report to the U.S. Senate, praising the Willamette as the finest grazing land in the world, claiming American ownership up to the Russian frontier at 54 40 , and urging protection for American settlers, and his report played its part in spreading "Oregon Fever," back east.

David Douglas

David Douglas was a sturdy Scotsman and a remarkable person. Before he was out of his 20's, he had traveled from his native land to the wilderness of the Pacific Northwest, where he made the botanical explorations that were to make him famous. It was he who gave his name to our Douglas fir tree.

Douglas arrived by ship to Fort George (Astoria) in 1823. He had been commissioned as a collector for the Royal Horticultural Society to collect any plants unknown by them and to record and ship some of them back to the British Isles. The gardens of Britain are filled with plants, trees and shrubs introduced from America by Douglas.

Douglas thought nothing of covering up to 50 miles a day on foot through the wilderness with a 50 pound pack on his back and his gun in his hand.

At Fort George, 12 miles upstream, Douglas was a little awed by his first glimpse of the man who was to be his host for the next year. Dr. John McLoughlin, chief factor of the Hudson's Bay Co., was a vigorous giant, standing six foot four, with a regal bearing, arrogant dark eyes, and a great shock of prematurely white hair. Douglas joined McLoughlin in coming from Fort George up to Fort

Vancouver. McLoughlin's plans called for a fort seven hundred fifty by five hundred feet square and twenty feet high, enclosing numerous log buildings.

Douglas made several trips upstream to the Cascades of the Columbia. Douglas hoped to gather a shipment of plants back with the "William and Ann" when she sailed in October. He adapted quickly to the new and rugged life, sleeping at night on a bed of pine or fir boughs or under brush, carrying only a little tea in a tin and depending solely on his rifle for food.

One evening about dark while returning down river, Douglas spotted a column of smoke rising in the forest near the river bank. Thinking it was a camp of voyageurs, or Canadian boatmen, he landed to join them. He failed to realize his mistake, until he found himself surrounded with more than a hundred braves; he had stumbled on a large Indian encampment.

Fortunately, Douglas had met their leader, Chief Cockqua, at Fort Vancouver and the chief invited him to join their feast. The Indians were eating sturgeon, a fish weighing five hundred pounds, which they had cut up and were roasting in the fires. Between sign language and the few English words that Cockqua knew, Douglas was able to carry on a conversation of sorts, but though the chief appeared friendly, the others watched Douglas suspiciously.

He learned that Cockqua's braves were preparing for war with the tribe across the river and after the feast almost three hundred warriors began to dance around the camp fires, leaping and goading themselves into a frenzy with their keening death songs. As the excitement mounted, from time to time a brave would dash into the light of the chief's fire and shake his weapons threateningly in Douglas' face. As Cocqua sat impassively studying his visitor, Douglas realized that he was being put to some kind of test. Finally, when many of the braves had dropped with exhaustion, Cockqua announced that it was time to retire and that if Douglas was afraid he could spend the night in his tent. Douglas suspected this was a test also and knowing the chief's tent would be full of fleas, he refused. With a nod of satisfaction Cockqua motioned to one of the Indians to throw Douglas a skin blanket.

Douglas was aware of the Indians watching him as he went about his preparations for the night. He built a bough shelter, lit a small fire, then opening his vasculum he took out a number of plant specimens and with great ceremony arranged them in a circle around his lodge as though they were a protective totem.

The Indians looked puzzled but seemed to understand. No one bothered him that night, but in the morning it was plain Cockqua was not yet ready to let Douglas leave. As a part of their preparation for battle, the braves staged an archery contest. When one brave had distinguished himself above all the others, Cockqua motioned that he now wanted Douglas to compete with this brave. A target was set upon a rock and Douglas hit it with the first shot from his gun. Unimpressed, the grinning brave did the same with his arrow. Next a target was suspended by a thong from a limb. Douglas hit this too; but so did the brave.

Just then a hawk flew overhead. Douglas raised his gun to his shoulder, there was a burst of feathers and the hawk dropped to the ground. Beside him, the brave grunted as though he had been kicked.

Cockqua smiled enigmatically, refusing to show whether or not he was impressed. He seized a high-crowned hat from one of the Indians and threw it into the air as though daring Douglas to repeat the feat. Douglas' shot ripped away the entire crown of the hat. Cockqua picked up the hat, stared at it in amazement, then shoved it down over the owner's head so far that his entire head came through. The Indians seemed to find this very amusing.

"The Grass Man is a great chief. The Grass Man is a medicine man like The Great White Eagle," Cockqua told everyone.

The Indians did not attempt to detain Douglas further and soon the title, Grass Man, had spread everywhere along the river. Just as the practical Indians could see no reason for McLoughlin to measure the river, they could see no reason for a man to collect plants he could not eat, so they concluded that this also had something to do with magical powers.

Douglas wanted to inspect the large douglas fir forest back of Beacon Rock. To climb the mountain he would need

44

a guide who knew the best route. Chief Chumtalia agreed to guide him wherever Douglas wished but when the chief learned that Douglas wished to climb the mountain he approached Douglas all doubled over, holding his stomach and grimacing in pain. Douglas suspected the attack was faked; the chief had hoped for some gifts but had no desire to climb a mountain in order to earn them. However, to spare Chumtalia's pride, Douglas pretended great concern for his health and accepted the services of two reluctant young braves the chief ordered to go in his place.

The braves had a good reason for their reluctant looks. Douglas traveled at a pace which his friends described as somewhere between a fast walk and a slow run, as he set off, the braves were hard pressed to keep ahead of him. All day they climbed, Douglas stopping only briefly to examine different plants. By dusk they had reached the summit, but it was too late to make their way back down at night. They had no food with them so Douglas lay down and went promptly to sleep. With several venomous looks in his direction, the shivering, hungry Indians did the same.

Douglas called the mountains the Cascades, the name they bear today, and became the first white man to climb to their summit. Not content with this feat, in the morning he went down the mountain, crossed the Columbia and the next day spent fifteen hours climbing the summit again on the south side below the rapids. He discovered the noble Fir.

In July of 1834, at 36 years of age, he met a tragic death in Hawaii. Intending to hike overland around the rim of Mauna Kea to Hilo. His only companions were a black man named John and a dog Billy. John was left behind on the way and Douglas asked a hunter who maintained wild cattle traps the way to travel. The hunter, Edward Gurney, warned Douglas of the traps in one of which was a bull. A few hours later Douglas' body was found at the bottom of the pit stamped to death by the enraged bull. He may have fallen into the pit while inspecting it.

By 1837, McLoughlin had farms at Fort Vancouver and on the Cowlitz River. American settlement in the Willamette Valley was discouraged.

1838—Senator Linn of Missouri brought in his Oregon bill proposing American military occupation right up to the

45

agreed frontier with Russia, at 54 40 North. He advocated the ending of the Convention for Joint Occupation west of the Rockies and the encouragement of American settlers by the grant of a square mile of land to each.

1841—Canadians were moving into the Willamette and totaled 350 against only 150 Americans.

1842—Dr. Elijah P. White came west with a party of 100 and with a commission from the Secretary of War of the U.S., to take charge of the Indian affairs west of the Rockies.

1843—875 more Americans came west and then they far outnumbered both the Canadians and the English, White announced that the American government meant to take the settlers under its protection. The Canadians held off any move to set up an American government. White set up a meeting at Champoeg in May where it was decided to set up their own provisional government. They adopted the Organic Laws and Articles of Oregon, based on the laws of Iowa, by a narrow majority.

The British and the Canadians were able to ignore the Organic Laws. Later McLoughlin gave his support to the formation of a temporary and provisional government. The need was to enforce law and order. The Provisional Government had no reference to the claims of the British and American governments, and it was agreed that it made no claims to any land north of the Columbia. But "Oregon Fever" could not be allayed so, President Tyler in his Message to congress in late 1843, claimed Oregon for the States with a boundary at 54 40 and with a chain of military posts to protect Americans from the Indians and English alike, and if necessary, to settle it with war.

In 1841 about 70 pioneers came by wagon train to The Dalles from Missouri. Over 100 more came in 1842. 1843 was known as "The Great Migration" when 1,000 immigrants left Independence, Missouri on the so-called "Oregon Trail", one out of ten died on the weary road; with about 850 of them finally reaching the Cascades on rafts or flatboats. Charles, Lindsay and Jesse Applegate, brothers, were in this group and each lost a son in the rapids when their boat overturned.

1844—The Parrott Family Came to Oregon—
   As told by Robert Parrott of North Bonneville

"After working on the Lake Erie Canal, Joseph Parrott in 1839 went to Frankfort, Kentucky. Soon he went from there to Andrew County, Missouri, met and married Nancy Kindred. There Joseph Jr. (my father) was born on January 18, 1844.

"The Kindreds were in Albermarle County, Virginia in 1886. The grandfather Kindred followed Daniel Boone to Kentucky.

"On the first day of May 1844, the Kindred family, including the Parrotts and Simmons, joined the Gillian caravan of Pioneers, and left Independence, Missouri, and headed across the plains and mountains, with Oregon City, Oregon as their destination. Along with the caravan was a free Negro and his family by the name of Bush. He was a big, husky man, very helpful and friendly, and very well liked by all members of the caravan, very few of whom he had not done some favor.

"The caravan moved quite slowly and had lots of troubles and delays. One time they came to a stream and made camp. During the night a storm came up and made the stream a raging torrent. They were there two weeks before they could cross, all because they did not cross the stream before making camp.

"When they got to the Blue Mountains it was getting late in the fall. The teams were all badly jaded, so they had quite a struggle getting over the mountains through an early snow, but they finally made it through the mountains to The Dalles. Joseph Parrott Jr. was just a babe in arms.

At The Dalles, the wagons were embarked on Hudson Bay Co. batteaus to Cascade, where they expected to get steamers to take them to Oregon City. There, most of them waited three weeks for a steamer. Food was scarce and a lot of them were hungry. Part of the emigrants drove the stock over some Indian trails that went south of Mt. Hood and to the Willamette Valley. They too were short of food, so when they camped for the night on a stream, and a stray dog came into camp, they killed and ate the dog, so they named the stream Dog River (Hood River).

"Joseph Parrott, being tired of the delay waiting for a boat at Cascade, made a project of his own. He took off his wagon box (prairie schooner), calked it water tight and used it for a boat to come on down the river, towing his wagon behind. The going soon got rough and he had to cut the wagon loose to keep it from swamping the boat. He stopped at an Indian camp where he expected to spend the night, and asked an Indian boy to bring him some fire, and he gave the Indian boy some powder for doing the same. Then came some older Indians, all hungry and begging for something to eat. One Indian refused the piece of meat offered and went to rummaging through things. To put a stop to that, Joseph picked up his gun and pointed it at the Indian. Suddenly, all the Indians but one jumped him, took away his gun, and made him pay dearly to get it back. Then the Indians left, all but the one, which Joseph figured had saved his life by motioning for him to leave, or the others would come back and kill him by cutting his throat. So they pulled out and made a camp on an island that night without any fire.

They all managed to reach Oregon City on the 23rd day of December, 1844, a crestfallen, discouraged, forlorn group of mortals, barely clothed in rags and moccasins, with no money or provisions, and winter coming on. It is hard to tell what might have become of them or been their fate, but for the generosity of Dr. John McLoughlin, who was factor at the Vancouver Hudson's Bay Company's well stocked store. He freely supplied their needs on credit, even though this act worked to his detriment later.

"Joseph Parrott soon took up a land claim about six miles south of Oregon City, near the east bank of the Willamette River where a small creek comes in. This creek is named Parrott Creek after him, and a small town on the highway where it crosses the creek, is named New Era.

"At this time things were getting pretty hot over slavery, as it was a few years before the Civil War. So, when they formed a government in Oregon, it was decided that no Negro would be allowed in the Willamette Valley. So what was to become of that free Negro Bush and his family?

David Kindred was a Southerner and hot headed, but with a fine sense of justice. He told those people in power there, that this Negro Bush "is just as good as any of you, and a damn sight better than most, and if he is not allowed to settle here, I'll be damned if I do either." So he gathered up as many emigrants as he could, and moved to what later became Washington Territory.

"He and his wife, his daughter Dollie and husband Mike T. Simmons, his son John, the Bush family, and many others went with him, and crossed over the Columbia and took up land claims at Tumwater.

"His son John and his son-in-law Mike Simmons, also located at Tumwater, and as partners, built a flour mill at the falls, the first in Washington. They used the falling water for power."

John C. Fremont, noted trail blazer, explored new routes into Oregon and California.

A British fleet of 16 vessels, mounting 350 cannon, was in the Pacific Ocean, in view of the uncertain status of the northern boundary.

The U.S. Frigate "Fisgard", 42 guns, and the "Cormorant", six guns, and the warship "America" were stationed at Puget Sound. November 2, 1845 the Man-of-War "Modeste", 18 guns, sailed up the Columbia River, anchoring near Fort Vancouver.

The British had noted the inflow of American settlers moving into the territory. Their ships could control ocean travel, but on the other hand these emigrants were traveling over the Rocky Mountains in large groups. 300 dragoons of the U.S. Regular Army having accompanied the last wagon trains. The Americans outnumbered the British 6 to 1 in the new territory. Lovejoy and Pettygrove had named the little city of Portland after Portland, Maine.

Barlow Road

In 1845 Joel Palmer crossed the Cascades from The Dalles to Oregon City with the Sam Barlow party. They suffered great hardships on the way, horses getting mired in the mud and wagons becoming stalled, sometimes requiring several teams doubled up to get each wagon moving

49

again.   The party included 19 men and women, 16 yokes of
oxen, 13 wagons, some drawn by horses.   The men slashing
brush ahead of the teams. Many of the hills going down were
so steep that trees were felled and tied on behind the wagons
to act as brakes.

Barlow received a franchise in 1846 allowing him to
build and maintain the Barlow Road and charge tolls of
$1.00 per head of stock and $5.00 per wagon.

The road was so poor that the legislature granted a new
franchise in 1852 to Hall and Hall who agreed to remove
stumps and rocks, put in bridges.   Later this year 1073
persons, with 673 wagons, 1396 horses and mules and 5680
head of cattle used the still very poor road.

Joel Palmer Pack Horse and Cattle Trail

In 1846 Joel Palmer established the Columbia River Pack
Trail, down the south bank of the river from The Dalles to
the Sandy River, for cattle.

1876 to 1878 the Palmer Cattle Trail was made passable
for wagons in summer time.

President Polk in his Inaugural Address in March 1845—

"Anxious to look the British lion in the eye", rallied
forth "Fifty-Four Forty or Fight."

In 1846, Texas and California were absorbed by the
United States, and on June 15, 1846, the Oregon Boundary
Treaty was signed. ·

La Prairie du

The Canadian fur trappers called the flat where Washougal
now is 'La Prairie du' from a species of wild mint which
grew there, and which was found a good substitute for tea.

Henderson Luelling's prairie schooner started west from
Indiana early in 1847 with an ox-team. He had 700 grafted
fruit trees packed in two boxes fastened to the sides of the

wagon. The boxes were filled with rich earth and were given good care on the journey.

On the North Platte, the wagon master urged Luelling to abandon his enterprise and leave the trees on the prairie as his oxen were getting footsore; Luelling then decided to travel alone. When he reached The Dalles the trees were floated down the Columbia on a flatboat and carried around the rapids at the Cascades, then floated down to the Willamette Valley, where he and his son started an orchard. They sold their first box of apples in Portland for $75, and four boxes brought $500 in San Francisco in 1851.

Cascade Mountains

The Cascade range of mountains came into existence during what is known as the Cascade Revolution, approximately one million years ago. The Cascade Mountains—a majestic north-south range of mountains extending from California through Oregon, Washington and into Canada. As the explorers passed from the east to the west of the Cascades, it was like entering another world.

Whether the name 'CASCADE' for these mountains originated from rapids in the river, or from the fact that numerous fine-spun waterfalls pitch from the steep sides of these mountains, is not known. It has been thought that David Douglas named these mountains "The Cascades" because of the waterfalls cascading down these mountains. During his travels, he identified more than fifty species of trees.

Indian Uprisings

The wagon trains trampled the grazing grounds and killed the game which the natives considered theirs. The Indians began to chafe at the intrusion of so many palefaces settling on their choice lands.

In 1847 a wagon train invested with measles stopped at the Whitman's Wailatpu Mission. Measles, being highly contagious, spread like wild-fire, first to a few whites at

51

the Mission and then to the Indians around the Mission. This was a new disease to the Indians for which their old standby cure did not work. The Indians used a sweat bath for many cures. They would build small huts with rounded tops, using small poles and then cover them with skins or blankets. A fire outside heated rocks which were placed inside the hut alongside the patient. The small size of the enclosure along with the hot rocks soon brought sweat out all over the sick one. If they had stopped right there things might have been different, but no, after half cooking the patient, he or she would dash out of the sweat-bath and plunge into a pool of ice-cold water. The sudden shock would either cure or kill some ailments but with measles it was a sure kill; as many as 5 per day died near the Mission.

A grave mistake was made by Mrs. Whitman. Chief Tamayhas came to the Whitman's home and he tried to give her a gift that the Indians prized. Two dried rabbit paws on a string which they thought would help ward off diseases with their primitive magic thoughts. Narcissa flatly refused the gift and shut the door in the Chief's face, a grave mistake.

Whitman Massacre

November 21, 1847 several Indians, including Tamayhas went to the Whitman's home under the pretext of inquiring for medicine. When the door was opened they killed Dr. Whitman with a tomahawk. The Indians then killed eleven men and Mrs. Whitman. Several of the residents escaped during the confusion but eight women, five men and thirty-four children were held as captives.

When word of this outbreak reached down the river the settlers went up in arms; the Federal Government had not passed any laws to protect the settlers; nor had they furnished one soldier to guard against hostile Indians.

The settlers then took things into their own hands and organized a regiment of volunteer riflemen to punish the Cayuse Indians and rescue the captives. These volunteer troops were to move to The Dalles under the command of Henry Lee.

The State Legislative Assembly passed a resolution for a bill providing for a messenger to take a plea to Washington, D.C. Joe Meek was chosen to be the messenger. Meek did not like some of the provisions of the bill because it required him to go east by way of California. It also required him to borrow $500 on the credit of the Oregon Territorial Government for the purpose of financing the trip.

Meek was an old experienced mountain man and he had his own ideas; during the wrangling with the politicians; Mr. Ogden, factor of the Hudson's Bay Co. at Fort Vancouver was taking steps to rescue these white people, the most practical way. He headed a party of Hudson's Bay men and on reaching the Cayuse country he let the Indians know that he was displeased with their doings and he bargained with them to release the captives for trade goods he had with his party. Ogden then returned to Fort Vancouver with the rescued captives. Three having died with the mistreatment of the Indians were buried before leaving. Among the ransomed was beautiful Lorinda Bewley, a white girl with blond braids, who had been kidnapped from a wagon train by Indian Chief Five Crows.

The first of the volunteers with Major Lee in command headed for The Dalles. He had orders to build a blockhouse, mounted with two guns at the Cascades, but with lack of provisions, he was forced to go on to The Dalles.

Joel Palmer, Commissary-General with more volunteers soon reached the Cascades with intentions of building the block-house but instead of a block-house they erected a few log cabins and named the place Fort Gilliam.

Major Lee was having his troubles at The Dalles trying to keep his volunteer troops from returning home. No food, guns, ammunition or heavy clothing had arrived, and it was the dead of winter.

January 8th. Scouts reported the Cayuses were rounding up livestock that had been put out to graze by the settlers, until warmer spring weather would make it possible to drive them over the mountains to the Willamette Valley. Lee ordered 17 of the poorly equipped volunteers to pursue the Indians and rescue the livestock. The Cayuse were on horses and volunteers were on foot. The Cayuse drove off 300 head of cattle while enjoying taunting the volunteers about being so unprepared and being afoot. However, the determined volunteers did kill 3 of the marauders.

Next day, Major Lee sent a detachment to see Chief Silelza of the Deschutes tribe, who had been robbed by the Cayuses because they had refused to join them. While in the area the volunteers captured 60 of the Cayuse's horses.

Colonel Gilliam arrived at the Cascades with 220 men. His troops were mounted on good horses but his provisions were sent to the Cascades by boat and had to be carried around the rapids, which delayed the troops considerably. While here, a messenger arrived from The Dalles telling of the skirmishes Major Lee had with the Cayuse.

On reaching The Dalles January 29, 1848, Col. Gilliam took 130 mounted troops and went as far east as the Deschutes River for the purpose of punishing the Indians who had driven off with the 300 head of cattle. He then sent Lee with some troops to scout for the Indians but they had seen him coming so were heading for the mountains. Lee attacked and killed one warrior and captured two women and a few horses. Lee's detachment while returning with his captives had to march through a ravine with high sides. Here the Indians coming around Lee's flank rolled large boulders down on the troops, but they managed to dodge the boulders.

Jan. 30. Gilliam joined Lee and the entire force started in pursuit, overtaking the Indians, the troops being mounted caused things to be different. They killed around 30 Indians and recovered several hundred dollars worth of stolen property, besides 4 head of cattle and 40 horses. The Indian camp was destroyed and burned. The older Indians who were unarmed were allowed to go free.

Palmer with more troops arrived at the Cascades and found the supplies at Fort Gilliam (the cabins), had been robbed.

Captain McKay arrived and they had a cannon with them. The two companies then resumed their march to The Dalles together. They arrived Feb. 10th and this established the forces of officers and men to 537. The Dalles was known then as Fort Wascopam.

Joe Meek had been Delayed

The redtape of elected officials had delayed Joe Meek three months. March 4, 1848 he started for the national Capitol. Meek and his party wore the caps and cloaks of the Hudson's Bay Company employees because it was much safer to travel through Indian country as a King George man than an American.

Col. Gilliam marched his troops into the Cayuse country hoping to catch the murderers of the Whitman Mission. The troops had marched all night and were pretty well fatigued when daylight came. Four hundred Palouse warriors had joined up with the Cayuse unknown to the Colonel, and Indians were everywhere. This is where the fiber of the volunteers stands out. They just kept coming on and pressing the Indians. The Indians filled the air with their war whoops and made a charge and they found the volunteers ready for fight. The volunteers yelled louder whoops than the Indians and kept right on coming. The Indians didn't stay long and lost four killed and fourteen wounded.

The Palouse deserted the Cayuse who fled into the Snake country where they were not welcome. The powerful Snake tribes would not let them remain. The Cayuse were tired of running and were unable to secure ammunition so the five murderers at Whitman's surrendered. Tamahas, Klakamas, Tiloukaikt, Isaiachalkis and Kiamassumpkin were now in the hands of the volunteers.

Oregon Becomes a Territory

August 14, 1848 a bill was acted upon in Congress, creating Oregon Territory; news traveled slow in '48, and it was five months before the news reached Oregon City.

October 26, 1848 Joe Meek arrived in Washington, seven months from Oregon City to the Capitol. He delivered his message and was informed that a sloop-of-war was being ordered to the Columbia River.

Joseph Lane was appointed as Governor and he arrived March 2, 1849. Joe Meek was appointed U.S. Marshal for Oregon Territory.

The new governor had the five captive chiefs brought to Oregon City. Every care was taken to give them a fair trial and when the jury was called, care was taken not to accept anyone who had had trouble with Indians. Trial was opened May 22, 1850 and on June 3rd a verdict of guilty was returned and execution ordered.

The badly pressed Cayuse Indians never recovered after their running into Snake country. In June 1851 an Indian Agent went east of the Cascades where he found a mere skeleton of the once powerful tribe; only 36 Cayuse warriors remained.

Cascades Portage Railroad 1851

Frances A. Chenowith, one of the early pioneers, was responsible for the northwest's first railroad.

He was an attorney from Wisconsin who came west in 1849 and located on a land claim on the north bank at the Cascades. He started a store at the Lower Cascades. J.A. Bush from Virginia was building a hotel and Putnam and Daniel Bradford, both merchants from Massachusetts were establishing a warehouse at the upper landing.

The Cascades being a natural obstruction which stopped all boats from passing it, canoes and bateaux had to be unloaded and everything they contained carried around the rapids. Chenowith, after watching party after party toil along the river bank with their precious belongings, decided there should be a better way to do this. The portage was two miles long over slippery, muddy trails.

He saw an opportunity for making money in building a railway portage. Mr. Bush helped him build a wooden railed tramway around the rapids. Wooden trestles across the gullies and alongside the bluffs, and ties laid on graded roadbed with wooden rails. A small flat car with a mule as a locomotive walking between the rails on a plank walk. Ready for business in July 1851.

For hauling freight the charge was 75¢ per hundred pounds. The passengers usually walked.

Some pioneers praised his initiative while some resented a charge being made. Two years later he sold out his interest to Bradford Brothers. However, Bush retained his share of the railroad. The railroad was extended to six miles in length by the new owners but mules and flat cars remained the rolling stock for several years.

The first portage railway was around the swift rapids where boats could not operate under any necessity. Below these "Hi-You Skookum Chuck" (very strong water) the river still ran too swift for the first steamboats for the next 4 miles. Safe to boat down but difficult to come up, often tow lines were needed with men on shore pulling, to enable the small boats and barges to get up as far as the lower end of the first tramway.

Mary Jane Hervey, born Nov. 7, 1820 in Muncy, Penn. was the daughter of Benjamin Elliott and Frances Holman Hervey. In 1847 she married John Williams in Nawco, Illinois.

Taken from the Attwell Letters

"We left for Oregon from Independence, Missouri, Feb. 26, 1852. We had a Conestoga covered wagon and a four-horse team and six cows with two calves. Some of the wagons were pulled with oxen, often 3 yokes to a wagon, when the wagons were heavily loaded as some were. On one wagon, besides the parents were six children, four of them too small to walk any great distance.

"Our boy Eddie (Charles Edwin) was 3 years old so he needed to remain on the wagon while the teams were moving. Sometimes I would take the reins from John and let him walk or hunt game for food. He was a good marksman and hunter. I walked as much as possible and helped others keep the cattle coming. There were 212 head of cattle, many of them milk cows with the train. Four young boys on their horses were a great help in herding the cattle.

"The wagon master, who was called 'Stud', I do not remember his real name but something like Studen or Studian, he was a good master. He set up wagon train laws that were lived up to. Murder was punishable with death. The penalty for stealing was a whipping with a black snake (ox whip) which would draw blood at every stroke. No one was put to death for a crime but two whippings did take place for not carrying out orders which endangered the train. Mostly, everyone was willing to help one another.

"The water was poor and the teams became weary so we were very glad to reach Fort Kearney—200 miles west of the Missouri River.

"So many animals either died or were killed along the trail or trains ahead of us, and were left unburied, the smell was terrible. Wolves followed the trains and ate on this carrion.

"Oxen were better than horses, not so high strung and would ford streams where horses balked. The Indians might stampede the horses at night but the oxen caused them more trouble.

"Cholera was dreaded more than the Indians. We would see as many as 20 new graves a day. We met many wagons returning with only women and children, their men were buried along the trail. The women and children were headed back to their homes in the east. This caused trouble passing another wagon going in the opposite direction.

"Pawnees attempted to stop our train and drive off the cattle. One Indian was shot. We wanted to get away from them but two families were very ill with cholera. The men were brothers, Will died, and Joe's wife died with two of their children. We buried Will and Nancy and the two children. Joe helped his sister-in-law harness her team along with his, so we got moving again.

"Many of the wagon train families brought along milk cows and they were milked morning and evening. Often extra milk would be placed into a milk can of 3 to 5 gallon in size and then tied to the wagon. After a day's journey over rough road it would churn to butter. We nearly always had fresh butter when camp was made late in the afternoons.

"In Wyoming the water was much better and John shot an antelope, which everyone enjoyed. The following day John became very ill so the wagon train laid over. John died that night and was buried not far from camp.

"I found my teams harnessed and hooked to the wagon the following morning; the neighbors on this wagon train were the finest people. Every evening I would unharness the teams, but they always came by and took my horses with theirs for the night, and bring them back in the morning and harness them for me.

"One evening two Indian boys, I guess I should call them young men but they seemed like boys, came by my wagon and gathered me some firewood so I gave them a little to eat. They could speak a little English. Eddie and I had our bed in the wagon but these two Indians slept on the ground near the fire. Before the camp stirred in the morning they were gone. The next 15 miles farther west about dark, here came these two Indian boys and they gave me some wild plums and then brought me some firewood. I again gave them something to eat.

"Stud came by and looked the Indians over and talked to them quite a while and then left. Next morning the Indian boys were gone, along with two of my horses. Several of the men mounted horses and made a search for them but they were miles away someplace.

"My wagon was too much for one team so here is where these wonderful wagon train pioneers always found a way to keep things moving. They brought two of my cows to the wagon and put the harness on them. The horse collars were placed upside down on the cows along with the hames. A horse pulls with his chest while a bovine pulls with its shoulders. The horse team would lead and still be driven with lines and the cows would tag along and help. This was pretty hard on the cows and the driver who tried to keep this combination going. A man named Nat Jones helped drive whenever I needed help, which was quite often.

"When we reached the Snake River it was too deep to ford so my wagon bed was a good one to calk up and use for a ferry boat. Some of the stock and men swam across, the ferry was called the 'Mary Jane'. Many things were left on the bank of the river and never ferried across.

"From Fort Boise on to The Dalles, about 350 miles of dust, lack of water and feed spent both teams and people. When the mess reached The Dalles, clothes all worn into rags, no food and many loved ones buried along the trail, we needed help.

"I sold everything including John's guns for $90 and got on the first flat boat that would take us. All we had was the rags on Eddie's and my backs and the $90.

"There were two families besides Eddie and me on the flat boat and it took us two days to float down the river to the Cascades. We were fortunate that it was August the 22nd when we reached here. The men beached the boat about one-half mile above the rapids on the north bank. Eddie and I were the first to reach Mr. Bush's house and hotel. The Bushs were some of the kindest people I have ever known. They took us in with open arms. I was now 8 and one-half months with child. September the 7th I gave birth to a baby boy at the Bush home. I named the baby Cassius Marcellus Williams. Eddie, born April 21, 1849, before we started from Illinois, was now 3 years and 5 months of age."

"Mr. Bush was 39 years old and his wife Julia was 33. They were from Virginia and she married him when she was 16. They had 5 children then and had two more later on. Besides their home they owned the hotel and hospital and were in partnership with Chenoweth on the tramway.

"The Bradfords had a warehouse and store near the Bush Hotel. Goods going up or down the river could be stored in the warehouse while waiting for boats.

"Many imigrants were coming down the river with always a delay encountered around the portage and the uncertainty of boats below the Cascades. The hotel, hospital and dining room were always crowded. Mrs. Bush asked me to stay there and help with the kitchen and dining room. I helped with the cooking and sometimes waited table and remained living in the Bush home. Their children watched over my two boys.

"I became acquainted with Roger Attwell when he came into the dining room to eat. He arrived at the hotel just 7 days after I did. He was a large man 33 years of age, six feet tall and weighing 200 pounds. He was a shipwright (boat builder) and had his tools with him. Mr. Bush wanted to build a steamboat to operate between the Upper Cascades and The Dalles, so he talked Roger into remainting there.

"Mr. Bush said, 'That man can take a broadaxe and square a log into a squared timber quicker than any ten men I ever saw do it. He stands on the log and swings that broadaxe within inches of his feet, squaring it down to size, then he takes an adz and finishes it as smooth as this table.'

"One evening when we were talking in the dining room and I had told him of losing the children's father, he looked at me and said, 'Lady, you need help. You can't make it out here without help with those two little boys. If you will marry me, I will help you.' This was an odd proposal, but, I knew that he was a good man, and I guess he knew from my smile that I was willing. We were married 6 months later."

Roger Gerard Attwell of Welsh parents was born in New York in the year 1821. He left Cincinnati, Ohio early in 1852 for Oregon. It is not now known who he came with or on what wagon but it is known that he brought with him over five hundred pounds of wood working tools. Many wagons were known to have lightened their loads along the way, throwing away stoves, chairs and even wedding dresses, so one wonders how he managed to bring his tools through. Wagons needed constant repairing on such a road as it was, so it may well be that tools of this kind were necessary, making new spokes for the wheels, wagon tongues or brake shoes and single trees or reach bars. If he had his own wagon and teams, they did not leave The Dalles as he came on down the river to the Cascades in a bateau, arriving August 29, 1852.

There he stayed at the Bush Hotel during the winter. He applied for a land grant of 320 acres where Cascade Locks is now located. He immediately went to work building a waterwheel powered sawmill and boatways for building steamboats.

Chief Chen O Wuth and 350 other Indians lived on this land. They remained friends and remained living on the land grant for many years.

Roger and Mary J. Williams were married the 18th day of May, 1853 at the Cascades, Clark County, Territory of Washington. The marriage license shows it as Oregon Territory because the justice of the peace had not yet learned that Congress three months earlier had made Washington Territory north of the Columbia River.

The Columbian...the first newspaper in Washington Territory chronicled up to the end of 1853...the marriage of twenty-two persons, the death of eight by disease, nine by drowning, one by falling of a tree, one by murder and two by suicide. Comparing dates it would have left the Attwells as the third white marriage in Washington Territory.

Roger Gerard Attwell
  Boat builder of the
  steamer Mary and other
  Columbia River boats

Mary Jane Attwell
  Bride of Roger
  1853

Letter by Mrs. J.C. Stille
  "Dr. Hiram A. Leavans was born in New York and in his teens went to Illinois. While there met a doctor who became interested in him, taught him all he knew of medicine and giving him his medical books. He worked as an apprentice and assistant to this doctor for a number of years. He married Pluma St. Ores and had two children, Turner and Em.

"1851...He decided to go west by wagon train, leaving his family with his mother in Illinois. He stayed in the west for eight years. During that time he filed on 160 acres just east of Castle Rock (Beacon Rock now) on the Columbia River. Building a house and planting an orchard. He was the only doctor on the Middle Columbia River so doctored many of the early settlers.

"He went east again by wagon train to his family and stayed there one year during which time a child, Anne, was born. He then organized a wagon train of which he was captain, and taking his family with him made his third crossing in 1860. They lived at Castle Rock for several years, then moved to Lower Cascades on the north bank. Another child, Ada, was born here.

"When the O.R. & N. Railroad was being built they moved into a houseboat and he put in a stock of dry goods and ran a store. The steamboat moved them occasionally. When he reached the rapids and could go no further, built a store building, moved his stock and opened a general mdse. store. He still practiced medicine for some time there and tiring of it, brought in an Italian doctor, Dr. Candiana to take over the practice."

Margaret Windsor arrives at The Cascades

"We landed in The Dalles in the year 1852 and came down the river on a raft to what is known as Shepard's Point.

"I had come down with mountain fever during the trip and was taken to the hospital which Mr. Isaac H. Bush had erected at the head of Cascade Rapids. He also owned a hotel, and I went to work for him as soon as I was able. Dr. Belford was the doctor at the hospital and he was a good doctor. While I lay sick in bed a new baby was shown to me who was Mary Williams' baby and named Marcellus. I wanted to hold the baby but I was so weak I couldn't. In later years everyone called him 'Celly', and he was a half-brother to J.F. and J.W. Attwell.

Celly

First white child born in
Skamania County

"While I was working for Mr. Bush at the hotel, I met and married Felix G. Iman.

"The Indians were getting more hostile and far enough to assure us of battle, so my husband decided he would move up on our donation claim about a mile distant. We had hewn logs and put up a house on what is yet known as Powder Island slough. We had decided to stay and fight off the warriors. We had carried in lots of wood and water and cut portholes through the walls of our house, making it a kind of a fort. We afterward abandoned this idea as there was a large pile of shavings from the shingles that lay against the house under the shed and on account of the underbrush which was close to the house, this would have been an easy mark for them to have thrown fire brands and cremated us while sleeping.

"While we were pondering over the situation, two hostiles put in an appearance about one hundred and fifty yards distance. They were huge and fierce looking. A man named Carter who was stopping at our house asked my husband if we had any guns, and he said, "Yes," and went out and brought two.

"Mr. Carter took one and my husband the other, each one of the men to name a warrior he was to shoot at, and Mr. Carter gave the signal to fire after good aim had been taken, but when the word was given my husband's gun made a long fire and he did not get his game, but Mr. Carter took his man square in the stomach. The other ran like an elk.

"They had fox skins filled with arrows and as they stood with bows on end they were almost as tall as the warriors, who were close to six feet. Mr. Carter got the bow and arrows."

First Steamer on the Middle Columbia

Mr. James P. Flint, a man with a little extra money, built the first small steamboat above the Cascades in 1851. It was named the "James P. Flint" and it was captained by Van Burgen. This little steamer was a little ahead of her need so it was decided to take her below the rapids. She hit a rock near Cape Horn and was sunk; later she was raised and her engines put into the new boat the "Fashion" and ran on the lower river until 1961.

The steamer "Allen" was built by the Hudson's Bay Co. in 1852 and in command of Captain Thomas Gladwell. She was wrecked on a dark night near Mitchell's Point just below Dog River (Hood River), two years later.

In 1851 the mail route, established in 1850 from Independence, Mo. to Salt Lake City was extended to The Dalles, in March 1851. Francis Chenowith contracted to carry the mail from Columbia City (Vancouver) to Cascade City (Lower Cascades) via canoe or boat along with operating his primitive railroad. It is not known how soon after the canoe mailboat that the mail was brought by steamboat; however, for thirteen years this was the only post office in Skamania County. Other postmasters operated the postoffice during these years. Daniel Bradford and Isaac H. Bush acted postmasters until 1863 when Samuel Hamilton became the postmaster.

Stevenson and Carson received their mail from Cascade Locks until 1894. J.P. Gillette was Stevenson's first postmaster, and Albert G. Tucker was Carson's first postmaster.

Two Donation Land Claims Filed on what is now Cascade Locks

John Chipman was born 1828 in Guilford County, North Carolina. He married Amanda M. Davis, November 27, 1851, in Adams County, Illinois. They arrived at the Cascades August 29, 1852, and filed for their claim February 15, 1853. Their claim ran along the south bank of the rapids from upper to lower ends.

The Roger and Mary Attwell's claim joined the Chipman claim and thence upriver approximately 1 mile.

Over 300 Indians remained living on the donation land claim and remained friends with their new landlords. Chief Chen o wuth and his wives often visited with Roger and Mary. He told them of Lewis and Clark coming down the river and that they camped on the island at the mouth of Rock Creek. He said that they crossed the river in 1805 and 1806 to visit his people.

(Whitehouse, one of the men with Lewis & Clark, wrote in his diary: "Wens. 30th. Oct. 1805. One half mile above the falls is a village of about 10 well looking cabins, covered with bark. These Savages were Surprised to see us, they thought that we rained down out of the clouds.")

Daniel Baughman took up a land claim here in 1852, which included the 7-1/2 acre island. Later he sold the island to Monroe Vallet and it became known as Monroe's Island. The waters from Bonneville Dam buried the island under water 75 years later.

Attwell took the Cascade Locks claim because of the fine timber on it. He built a sawmill on what is called Attwell Creek. This was before circular saws were in use, so he used the SASH saw. This large straight saw worked up and down, much like a hand saw in a carpenter's hand. It was powered by a large overshot waterwheel. A skid road was built to the mill and the saw logs were brought to the mill with yokes of oxen.

A boat 'way' was made on the shore of the claim and several steamboats were built here, the "Mary" the first. The "Mary" was a side-wheeler, 77 feet in length with tonnage of 97 tons. Mr. Bush ordered her built and paid the

67

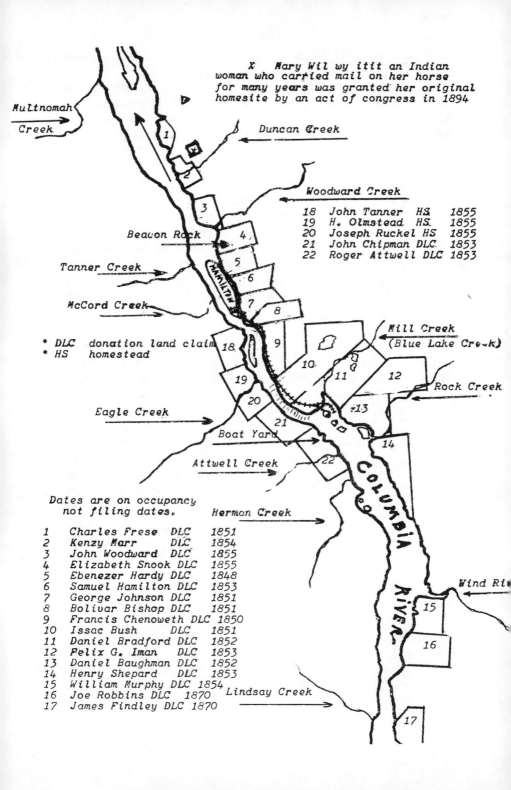

NOTIFICATION TO THE ~~SURVEYOR~~ GENERAL OF OREGON, OF SETTLEMENT
ON PUBLIC LANDS NOT YET SURVEYED.

Pursuant to the act of Congress approved on the 14th **day** of February, 1853,

entitled "An act to amend an act entitled 'An act to create **the office of SURVEYOR**

GENERAL OF THE PUBLIC LANDS IN OREGON, and to provide for the survey and make

donations to settlers of the said public lands,'"

I, *Roger G Attwell* a *free white man*

age 34 years was married to Mary J Williams on the

18th day of May 1853

of *Wasco* county, in that part of the TERRITORY OF OREGON now

established as the TERRITORY OF ~~WASHINGTON~~ *Oregon*, hereby give notice of my claim to a

DONATION of *320* acres of land, particularly bounded and described

as follows: Beginning at *large balm a giliad tree*

36 inch in diameter situated a short

distance above the Columbia falls

in Oregon this corner ~~tree~~ stands by the

mouth of ~~a small stream~~ that empties

in the Columbia River this corner tree

~~being both~~ ~~line~~ ~~between~~

John Chipmans Claim & my Claim

from thence running up the River

about one mile to a small fir tree

that stands on a large pile of stones

thence back

Roger G Attwell

L. S.

Roger G Attwell of *Wasco* county, in the
Territory of ~~Washington~~ *Oregon*, being first duly sworn, says that he is a white settler on the
public lands in that part of Oregon now established as the Territory of Washington,
and that he arrived in Oregon on the *29th* day of *August*, 185*2*,
and was a resident thereof on and before the first day of December, 185*2* that he
is a *married man*

and that he was born in *New York* county, in the
year *1821*; that he ~~has personally resided~~ upon and cultivated that part of the
public lands in that part of Oregon now established as the Territory of ~~Washington~~ *Oregon*
~~particularly~~ described in the ~~annexed notification~~ to the Surveyor General of Oregon;
continuously, from the *12th* day of *April*, 1853, to
the *1st* day of *April*, 185*3* And he further says
that he is intermarried with *Mary J Williams* his wife; and that he was
legally ~~married~~ to her on the *18th* day of *May* 18 *53*,
in *Skamania* county, in *Washington Territory*

Subscribed and sworn to before me,
this *1st* day of *April* 18 *55* *R G Attwell*
in *Skamania Co*
Washington Territory

L.S. *Jas E More clerk*
Dist court

costs. It is not quite clear when the Bradford Brothers became part owners. The launching date was September 12, 1853, and a big celebration was held aboard the boat.

The Wasco was completed on these same ways in 1855 for Mr. McFarland. McFarland was captain and his son Cornelius, the engineer. This boat was a side-wheeler like the "Mary".

One of the first things needed to start building a steamboat was the bow stem. Nowadays a bow stem is laminated into the right curve. Then it was necessary to find a large tree growing on the mountainside, fell the tree, dig out the right shaped large root and then saw down through the stump alongside the root to be used. This stem, shaped something like a boomerang, was then hauled out of the woods with a yoke of oxen down to where the steamer was to be built. Two brothers made a business of hewing out these boat stems for a number of years. They received $175 a stem.

1853 A request was made to Major Rains for forming Wasco County with boundaries running from the Cascades (Cascade Locks) south to the California line, thence east along this line to the Rocky Mountains thence north to the Columbia River and west to the Cascades. The major turned down the request with saying, "It is too large a territory for only 35 white people in the area."

Later Wasco County was created January 11, 1854, and took in all Oregon territory from the Cascade Mountain Range to the Rocky Mountains. It was named for an Indian tribe in the area.

Lt. George B. McClellan arrived at the Cascades with a party of men for the purpose of exploring the Cascade Mountains in the interest of the Northern Pacific railroad. His main object was to find, if possible, a feasible pass through this mountain range. In his exploring a cannon was buried near the huckleberry fields back of Carson. Treasure hunters are still looking for the olde cannon 120 years later.

This was the envelope for the following
letter written in 1853 by Mr. Attwell
at the Cascades to Mr. Chenoweth at The Dalles.

Sep 8th 1853

Dear Sir.
You will oblige me very much
If you While do me a favour which it seems
impossible for me to attend to as I am very
busy building a steamboat for Mr Bush
and would not have time to attend to it
the favour that I would ask of you is for
you to purchase for me a whale boat that
belongs to Mr Gibson which is now sunk at
the dalls The Same boat that I repaired
the reck of which belonged to goverment
Mr Gibson has offered it for 30 dollars
for some time back but no Buyers I want
you to get it for me as cheap as you can
& I will settle it with you I want it to

Cross the river in as I have lost my Canoe
If have not time to Make me another Convey me
as sootoble as the one under Consideration
I would like you to get it as cheap as you Can
If not to Give over 40 or 50 dollars for it
I oblige Yours. Give My respects to your wife
& accept the same for yourself

R. G. Attwell

Please send Me a note by Mail assoon
as most Convenient I oblige Gerry
respectfully Yours

R. G. A

SHEPARDS
Recollections of Elizabeth R. Holtgrieve

I was born October 26, 1846, in Jefferson County, Iowa, at a place called Brush Creek, about fifteen miles from Rome. My father, Henry Shepard, was a pioneer to Iowa in 1837. The Indians were there at that time but later they moved to Minnesota. Two years later my father's father, Charles Shepard, his mother, Sarah Springstein Shepard, and three brothers, Charles, James and Joseph, moved from New York to Iowa. Father's birthplace was Dewaynesburg, Schenectady County, New York, and my mother, Elizabeth Mattern, was born November 14, 1811, at Hesse-Darmstadt, Germany. She died a week before Christmas in 1849, and in the fall of 1851 my father, with my sister and me, his brother Joseph and wife Loisa, and two other young men started for St. Joseph. One of these men was Ellis Straway and the other Martin Huffman.

When we arrived at St. Joseph, they took the cattle across the Missouri River to winter. We had two wagons, three yoke to a wagon, three cows and one horse. The three men worked for an Indian agent that winter. This man was named Pensonmaw. The cattle wintered themselves on the big rushes which grew in that country, and it happened to be a mild winter, such as I have seen many times in Oregon. My aunt stayed with the men and did their cooking while my sister worked for different families most of the time. I stayed with the family named Hannah, who came from Iowa with us. In the spring my uncle felt discouraged and with Ellis Straway and Mrs. Hannah and her three children all started back to Iowa by boat, by way of St. Louis and Kerkirk. My father, sister and I, with Martin Huffman, fixed to start for Oregon. Three other men hired out to come with us for $10 each. One man furnished one ox to drive in a yoke. They brought the cattle over the river to St. Joe and put them in a corral so as to have everything prepared for our long journey, but when we were ready to start father found that three of our cows had been stolen.

We started the 27th of April, 1852, and traveled up the Missouri to Kansas City and there crossed over in a ferry boat. Before we crossed the river we joined another train

of emigrants.   The captain of that train was named Dr.
Bonner; he had a half-brother named Eddy, who acted as
captain when his brother was waiting on the sick.   We
traveled up the Missouri two days when we met two men
with a team of horses who were on their way to California.
We traveled about two weeks on the plains and everything
was fine.   One night three Pawnee Indians came to our camp
and stayed all night and slept under one of the wagons.   We
gave them their breakfast and they went away, but the next
evening they came back and stayed that night also.   The
third night they came back and stampeded all the horses,
about seven head, and we never did get them back.   Mr.
Kane bought another team from the French traders and
came on with us until he came to the road to California.

A great many people suffered with cholera, but we only
had two cases in our train.   The first was a little girl, two
years younger than myself.   She and I were great friends
and playmates.   Her name was Elmira Eddy. I remember
the morning she was taken sick.   They stopped the train and
my father, being a doctor, stayed with them.   He did not
overtake us until we had arrived at the last crossing of the
Platte River.   He borrowed the captain's horse and overtook
us before daylight.   They were fixing the oxen to cross the
river, but father told them they could not do that until the
captain overtook us.   They insisted, however, until another
campman said, "No, you must wait."   So they decided to do
so.   Then one of our men, Martin Huffman, took the cholera.
The three men did all they could to save him.   Happily they
saved him and he came on to Oregon with us.

We did not have any more trouble until we came to the
California road.   Some of the men wanted to go to California,
but father said, "No.   I started for Oregon and I am going."
The men stayed with us until we arrived near The Dalles,
when they packed their things and started on afoot.   When
we were within five miles of The Dalles, we camped by
another party. A most pitiful sight awaited us: some children
named Fitzgerald had lost father and mother on the plains.
I stayed at camp and cooked my own dinner the day I was
twelve years old.   My father had married again in September
at Fort Boise to a Miss Louinda Nelson while we were on
our western journey.

At The Dalles my father and stepmother went to see some people off on the boat to Portland. My sister went to the Cascades with a family named Coston. My father, my stepmother and myself stayed in The Dalles that winter. We had a very hard winter with lots of snow. Another family by the name of Gardner stayed with us in the hospital. They later settled on the Lewis River, Washington.

When the spring opened, my father took a place two miles below The Dalles. It was a pretty spot, grassy and very level with oak trees scattered about. Near by about 300 yards of Mill Creek. There was a big Indian camp about a quarter of a mile above the place. The chief's name was Mark. My father had spaded the ground and had quite a little garden growing, when the chief went to Major Alvord and made a complaint against us. He said we were on his ponies' grazing ground. He said if we would go peacefully he would send Indians to help carry the things down to the river, so father was notified the next day by the government. The soldiers and Indians came and helped move our household goods down and we stayed there four days. A flat boat came up the river under the management of Captain Baughman. Father went to The Dalles to see him about taking us down to the Cascade Falls. We started for a place now called Council Crest, where my stepmother's people had taken land back in the hills. When we arrived at Captain Baughman's house, a mile above the falls on the Washington side, we stayed all night. The captain said it looked like rain and we had better carry the things up to his house, which the men did. The next morning it was raining, and continued for two or three weeks. The good captain proposed for us to stay at his house until he made a trip to The Dalles. We stayed there while he moved two families. One named Smith went to the Grand Ronde country, and the other was Joslyn who settled at White Salmon and started a stock farm, living there for many years.

When the captain returned he took my father to look at a land claim two miles above the Cascades (where Stevenson is now). When my father got back, he said he would take it as it had the most wonderful timber he had ever seen. The captain told him he could make a good living by cutting the wood and sending it to The Dalles. So we moved up. It was the last of April, 1853, and father found work that summer where Cascade Locks is now. He helped in building a steamboat for Mr. Bush. He worked until September when the boat was ready to be launched. All the people in the neighborhood were there. They gave a wonderful dinner. It was the first celebration ever held at the Cascades, September 12, 1853. That fall my father hired men to cut logs and build a log house. We lived in a tent all summer but moved into our new house in December. Then father hired men and they cut wood and banked it near the river to sent to The Dalles.

My sister was married to Francis M. Vanderpool, January 24, 1853, at the Cascade Falls, Washington, at the home of Mr. and Mrs. Bush. She worked at the hotel when they were married. She came up to The Dalles on the first boat to visit us. When we took our place, they went back to the Cascade Falls. In June, Mr. Vanderpool went to the Umatilla country while my sister went to Portland to work. After three years he came back, and together they took up a place where the Stevenson cemetery now is. It is now known as the old Bevans place. It was one place above my father's and was first known as the Vanderpool place.

(Recollections of Elizabeth Holtgrieve will be continued later.)

March 1853. Congress created Washington Territory, separating from Oregon Territory all north of the Columbia River. The news of this had not reached the Cascades until late in May.

Major Isaac Stevens was appointed governor but did not arrive in the new territory until September 29, 1853. The new governor crossed overland from East to West.

The population of the new territory was less than 4,000 white people. Eleven people lived in Tacoma and about one hundred in Olympia at this time.

The steamer "Columbia" made a monthly trip from San Francisco to Portland carrying mail and passengers. Rates: $90.00—1st cabin; $45.00—Steerage. Flour was $15 per bbl.; Ham 40¢ a lb.; salt pork $40.00 a bbl.; butter 75¢ a lbs.

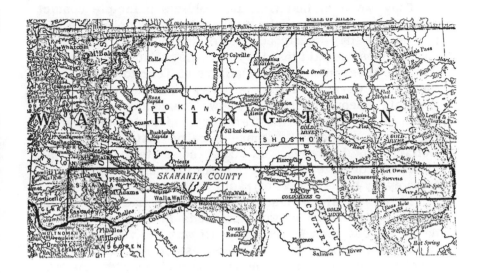

1853—AN ACT TO CREATE AND ORGANIZE THE COUNTY OF SKAMANIA.

Sec. 1. Be it enacted by the Legislative Assembly of the Territory of Washington, That all that portion of Clarke county lying east of Cape Horn, be and the same is hereby organized into a county, with all the powers, rights and privileges of other counties in the territory; and that it shall be bounded as follows: commencing at a point due north of a rock on the south bank of the Columbia River, called Rooster Rock, running thence north to the parallel of 46 deg. 30 minutes north latitude, thence along said parallel east to Rocky mountains; thence along base of Rocky mountains to south east corner of Territory of Washington; thence down along the line of Oregon and Washington territories to place of beginning.

Sec. 2 Said county shall be called Skamania.

Territorial legislatures established powers and duties of a board of commissioners for the new counties in 1853; it was changed to function under statehood in 1889.

They were at that time the public's principle contact with government, its only means of making collective will felt in the day-to-day conduct of the public's affairs. It could almost be said that they were the public's only contact with the government, for the affairs of Territorial Government then were vastly farther away from the daily lives of the state's people than they are now. The county was government in the days of the Territory, so far as the general public was concerned. There were no state programs in welfare, in highways, in taxes; no state police or tax collectors or state officials broadcasting thunderous orations from every home's T.V. or radio.

To cite a single instance, these men had to build and maintain the entire network of roads in the Territory and do it without even a tax levy! (It was two years later, at the second Territorial legislative session in 1855, before a specific levy for road construction and maintenance was adopted.)

The members of the first board of county commissioners had been elected on staggered terms, one man for one year, one for two years and the third commissioner for a three-year term. Terms of their successors were all to be three years, preserving the staggered pattern of vacancies to be filled by annual elections.

They were required to hold four sessions each year, meeting at the county seat (Cascades City) on the first Mondays in April, July, September and December. The regular sessions could last no longer than six days. Their compensation was set at three dollars per day for time spent in meetings or on other official business, plus 10 cents per mile for travel. (But the legislature took no other chances with this one—they required all such travels to be computed "by the most usual traveled route".)

In 1853, the Assessor was an official elected in each county for one year. His job was to determine the amount of assessed valuation which should be carried on that county tax roll. He also took the census, kept the county plat book and certified the list of those eligible for the militia.

The Assessor was required to collect a county pole tax of $1 from each male inhabitant between the ages of 21 and 50. He kept 10% of all the money collected as his fee. Legal voters were those persons who were either over fifty years of age, or those who had paid a poll tax.

The Commissioners were charged with the exclusive care of the poor in their respective counties under rigid rules established by the legislature. If an indigent had relatives, the Commissioners were to order one or more of them to support the indigent person if they were financially able to do so; if those persons refused, then the commissioners were authorized to recover in the courts from any direct relative (father, mother, sister, brother, grandfather, grandmother or grandchild) the sum of $30 per month for the indigent's care.

There was a provision that a man might work on the county roads in lieu of paying taxes.

The Commissioners were also a sort of legislative dumping ground. If some legislator happened to know of a problem that had no solution under Territorial government readily available, he frequently suggested turning it over to the board for disposition. For example, if anyone found a strayed animal, he was to take care of it and notify the clerk of the board that he had it. If the owner could not be located, the animal was to be sold and the proceeds divided equally between the finder and the County Treasurer. A similar arrangement was worked out for lost money and goods.

The Treasurer was elected for a two year term, to receive and disburse all county moneys. He was to keep account books in such a fashion that the amount received and paid out would be shown. When county orders were presented to him, if there was not enough money in the treasury to pay them, he would endorse each order so that it would draw interest until it could be redeemed by the county. The Treasurer received 2% on all moneys taken in and another 2% on all money paid out; this was his fee.

In the 36 years between that first session in 1853 and Statehood in 1889, the Territorial Legislature changed its mind many times about the way it wanted its creatures, the counties, to do things. For example, the fees the legislature allowed county officials to charge the public for their services continued as late as 1877.

Sometimes the Sheriff was ex-officio the County Assessor. Things rocked along like that (confused as they must have been) until Statehood in 1889.

The counties themselves were not too well organized as yet, either. In 1877, the legislature was told by the Territorial Auditor that he figured over $21,000 was due the Territory for Territorial taxes and that he was unable to settle the matter through correspondence. So the legislature ordered the Auditor to send a transcript of his version of the account to the Prosecuting Attorney of the judicial district in which the county was located, and have him reach agreement with the local County Auditor as to the amount due, which was then to be paid forthwith.

Four years later, however, the legislature found that, although the Territorial Auditor had shown "due diligence" in trying to make the settlements, he had been unable to do so because of the imperfect manner in which the county records were kept. So the legislature ordered him to figure out how much each county owed; make an entry in his books crediting each with the amounts; balance his books; shut up, and let everybody forget about the whole thing.

The Commissioners were further directed to divide their counties into convenient road districts and to appoint annually at their April session a supervisor of roads in each district, who was to be responsible for keeping the roads in that district in good repair. The supevisors were to list the names of all persons liable to the performance of road work—which meant every able-bodied man between 18 and 50 years of age, except ministers, residing in the district. Each of these persons was to perform a basic three days work each year. The supervisor received $3 per day for time spent on the road in his district. This post of supervisor could not have been a very popular one, for the early statutes say that whoever was appointed to fill the post had to serve under penalty of fine. The only compensation for this harshness was the additional statement that no person could be forced to serve for more than one term!

The Yakima Indian War

Governor Stevens visited Walla Walla in June 1855, presenting treaties with the Kootenai, Pend Oreilles and Flathead nations. After success with these tribes, he prepared to return down the Columbia.

A messenger arrived informing him of a full swing war in progress by the Yakimas and that he would be in great danger attempting travel through hostile territory. The friendly Nez Perce offered to escort the governor safely through to The Dalles. Another messenger arrived informing the governor that the trustworthy Oregon Volunteers had met the Yakimas in a fierce battle and Chief Peu-peu-mox-mox had been killed.

Governor Stevens now knowing that the Yakimas were too busy fighting with the volunteers for him to need a large escort; so he set out the next day with 69 young Nez Perce warriors and a few miners wanting to get down river.

He met Indian Agent B.F. Shaw, who was also a Colonel in the volunteer army of Washington Territory. The governor ordered the colonel to form a company of home guards to protect the settlers and friendly Indians around Walla Walla. He also ordered that the 69 friendly Nez Perce receive payment for their escort services and to return to their homes with Shaw. Governor Stevens went on down the river to the Cascades, spending one night at the Bush Hotel and then going on to Olympia.

The Governor was welcomed home because Indian troubles were causing great concern on Puget Sound. Settlers on the White River had escaped an Indian attack by hiding in the underbrush. Next morning all the settlers hastened to Seattle.

A detachment under Lt. Nugent with his soldiers marched through the White River district and are assured by the local Indians that no trouble existed. Returning to Seattle he informed the nervous settlers that all was all right and that they should return to their homes. On Oct. 28th those that returned home were massacred.

Captain Hewitt, with his troops of volunteers went to the White River Valley to bury the dead.

Lt. W.A. Slaughter was ordered to take his troops into the White River Valley. On November 25th his force was attacked during a dense fog, by Klickitats, Nisquallies and Green River Indians. One soldier was killed and 40 of the troop's horses were stolen.

Dec. 4th, Lt. Slaughter and Capt. Hewitt were conferring in a cabin when Lt. Slaughter was shot and instantly killed by a lurking·Indian who shot through he window of the cabin. A little town located here at the site was named 'Slaughter', and was later changed to 'Auburn'.

The sloop-of-war "Decatur" came into Puget Sound. Governor Stevens returned to Olympia on January 19, 1856, friendly Indians warned of the trouble to come from hostile Indians. January 25th the hostiles came by way of Lake Washington. The men from the ship "Decatur" spent the night ashore on guard duty. Before they could have breakfast the next morning an alarm sounded. The battle raged until ten that night. Two white men were killed and an unknown number of Indians. The hostiles left in defeat but they sent word that they would be back with enough warriors to take Seattle even with their man-of-war.

The "U.S.S. Massachusetts" arrived at Seattle in February and the "U.S.S. John Hancock" in March 1856. This did much to convince the local Indians that there was force to meet. However, hostile Indians came down from the north and were met by some of the forces from the ships. They refused to return home so hostilities broke out. Twenty-seven Indians were killed, twenty-one wounded out of a total of 117 warriors. Their canoes and supplies were destroyed and the survivors were transported back to Victoria Island aboard the Massachusetts.

The volunteers hunted down the ring leaders among the hostile chiefs. Much of the cost was defrayed of these volunteers by auctioning off the animals captured from these Indians. Washington Territory was taking its place in the roster to be recognized by Congress.

The volunteers in the Walla Walla Valley were having terrific hardships. It was 20 degrees below zero with snow everywhere. Their clothing was worn thin, shoes were worn out and the men improvised moccasins from rawhide. During this time, two of the companies were busy recovering property stolen from the immigrants. The troops were anxious to be relieved and return to their homes.

This living and cooking their meals in a thin tent in sub-zero weather was wearing their nerves thin.

The Walla Wallas whom the troops were to guard, slipped out in the dark of night December 5th and had headed into the country north of the Snake River. The volunteers could not go after them as there were no boats, so several weeks were spent in making six boats.

March the 7th, the regiment crossed the river and a few Indians opposed them but were soon repulsed with some casualties and loss of their horses. The horses were slaughtered for food. The troops proceeded northeast for several miles. The land was very poor with little grass so many of their own horses died and they spent several days rounding up Indian horses to remount the troops.

The troops returned to the Walla Walla Valley. There was a shortage of food and supplies. Colonel Cornelius was so concerned about the inadequate commissary that he set out for The Dalles with part of his command. His route was along the north bank of the Columbia and, about 60 miles down river, he was attacked by 300 warriors of Chief Kamiakin from Yakima. The Indians were repulsed and the troops could not pursue the Indians because of their short supplies.

Five miles above The Dalles while making camp the Indians stampeded the horses leaving the troops afoot.

The Federal Army with all its red tape was finally being made ready to relieve some of the volunteers. General Wool, a very unpopular general, sent Colonel Wright to command the Columbia River district with his eight companies of soldiers.

Colonel Wright took his time, remaining in Vancouver for several weeks. In early March, Colonel Wright began moving his troops to The Dalles. This caused a large quantity of army supplies to be piled up at the Cascades.

A blockhouse was erected between the lower and upper landing. Eight men under Sergeant Kelly were left at this blockhouse. March 24th the main company of soldiers left the blockhouse for The Dalles on board the steamer "Mary". On the morning of March 26th the Yakimas and a few Klickitats attacked the upper landing and the blockhouse.

85

Told by Mrs. Mary Attwell

"March 2nd, 1856. Mum-shum-sie, wife of Chief Chen o wuth came to our house to warn us. She said, 'Chief Chen o wuth wants me to tell you that some Yakima Indians are in our village. He told them to not go near your home or bother you, but he does not know if they can be trusted. He thinks that it would be best if you took your 3 boys and hid in the woods until they went by.'

"Roger was away, so I took the three boys, Eddy was 6, Celly 3, and James Fremont (Monty), 1 year old, we hurried across the field into a thicket. We could still see Mum shum sie walking back toward her home, when she darted into the tall hay and laid down out of sight. In a moment here came about 20 warriors not far from where we were hidden. They were not from our local village, were taller and all armed with guns. Celly wanted to talk, 'What's at?' and when I held my hand over his mouth he cried. The strange Indians were talking among themselves so did not hear Celly, and they did not go to the house. If they had seen Mum shum sie they might have considered her a spy and punished her.

"Chief Chen o wuth was a good man and this was the first time that we needed to leave our home. Over 300 Indians lived near our home and we trusted them and they trusted us."

These strange Indians may have had canoes somewhere above on the river and returned back to the north bank to burn the Joslyn home.

The Oregon Portage

Joseph S. Ruckel leaving New York in 1845 was one of the first settlers to cross the Isthmus of Panama, there he caught the U.S. Sloop "Preble" and sailed for Yerba Duena, as San Francisco was then called. He remained there for nine years and ran a store. He came to Oregon in 1855 and took up a homestead just upriver from Eagle Creek. He built a home here.

Across the river on the north bank was the little portage railroad operated by Bradford & Company. Wooden rails, and wooden cars drawn by mules, crude as it was, it was a big money maker. Chenoweth who had built the portage in 1851 charged 75¢ per hundred pounds, but Bradford & Company doubled the price when they purchased the portage from the former owners. Considerable dissatisfaction grew in Portland and elsewhere at these exorbitant charges. Regardless of the high charges on the portage, business increased. Gold mines discovered in eastern Washington and Oregon gave a vast increase in business over the portage, and the Government poured a steady stream of supplies to the soldiers stationed at The Dalles and above. Money poured into the new owners' pockets so they started rebuilding the 2-1/2 mile tramway and extending it to a full 6 miles, to what became known as the Lower Landing which was below the swift water.

Harrison Olmstead took a land claim joining Ruckel's west boundary, this claim extended one mile further down the south bank and included Eagle Creek and Tooth Rock.

Bradfords had taken a claim on the large island off shore on the south bank, in an effort to preclude opposition. This island became named Bradford's Island.

Ruckel and Olmstead decided to put in a portage on the south bank of the river, so they formed a partnership. The new partnership interested Captain VanBergen into joining with them and buying the steamer Fashion from the Williams, it would run between Portland and the new Oregon Portage.

McFarland of The Dalles was building the steamer "Wasco" at the Attwell boatyard above the Rapids, and would run between the upper end of the new portage and The Dalles.

W.R. Kilborn joining the partnership was busy with his teams making a road around the rapids on the south bank.

The following ad appeared in the Oregonian:
"PORTLAND, CASCADES AND THE DALLES"
"The undersigned having made arrangements for transportation of Freight over the Portage at the Cascades on the Oregon side, and having the necessary teams, boats, etc.; will receive and transport with the upmost dispatch all Freights, Goods, Wares and Merchandise by the steamers Fashion and Wasco and other companies. The road is now in complete order. My teams will always be in readiness.

87

Good warehouses have been erected and my personal attention given to business.

W.R. Kilborn

Feb. 9, 1856   Lower Cascades, Oregon Side"

Colonel Ruckel with good business ability and lots of energy secured a transportation contract with the Government March 8th for transporting their supplies from Fort Vancouver to The Dalles. He became an agent for the Quartermaster Department.

The Bradford Company was using the Side-Wheeler the "Belle" on the lower river, she was 54 tonnage and 96 feet long, and the "Mary" on the middle river. Ice blocked the river from bank to bank as far as Vancouver. In February the ice broke up and the "Fashion" and the "Belle" started bringing freight to the lower landings. On the North Bank, ox teams took the freight through axle deep mud from the lower landing up to the mule-powered railway. On the south bank the portage was only a footpath for pack mules and passengers.

SAPOTIWELL (1856)
(Also known as Johnson)

(Data furnished by Mrs. Camilla Donnell, mother of Lulu D. Crandall of The Dalles.)

In 1856 the Joslyn family was the only white family living east of the Cascades, on the Washington side of the Columbia River.

The town of Bingen is located on land owned by them and the home of Judge Byrkett is not far from the site of their cabin.

The Yakima and Klickitat Indians plotted to destroy their property and murder the members of their household, but Sapotiwell, a friendly Indian, disclosed the plot to Mr. Joslyn and he and his wife went to the Cascades where Mrs.

Joslyn remained to visit with Mrs. Attwell, whose home was on the Oregon side (now the Cascade Locks), while Mr. Joslyn attended to some business at The Dalles. Mr. Galentine, an experienced frontiersman, remained on the Joslyn farm to care for the stock, with Samuel Woodburn Hawkes, a fourteen year old orphan boy, as companion and helper. The Indians were greatly incensed at the escape of Mr. and Mrs. Joslyn and planned to take vengeance on Sapotiwell, who fled to the Oregon shore, taking every boat with him. A few days later, at milking time in the evening, Mr. Galentine heard the voice of an Indian woman calling softly to him from the willows nearby; driving the cow near the willows he continued his milking while she revealed to him that the Indians were then on their way to murder him and his companion. Quietly he turned the cows and calves together, called Sammy, and taking his gun, made his way to the river's edge where the willows were the thickest.

A night of terror followed, a band of blood-thirsty Indians scoured the thicket but the white man and boy eluded them although the Indians came very near them on several occasions. When morning dawned The Dalles boat came down the river and was hailed by the refugees at a point of land opposite Mosier. Mr. Galentine and Sammy were taken aboard and landed at the Coe farm.

The Indians regarded Sapotiwell as a traitor and only waited their time to wreak vengeance upon him, so Sapotiwell remained with the whites, helping them on all occasions. He changed his name to Johnson and became a welcome guest in the homes of the pioneers who appreciated his sacrifice.

AMOS UNDERWOOD AND FAMILY D.M.C. 1852
(From Coe Diary, "Central Oregon", A. Underwood)

September 9th, 1852, is the date given by Mr. Underwood as the time when he first came to "Dog River". This was before the arrival of the Farnsworth and Laughlin families, and he was probably on some business and lived either at The Dalles or at the Cascades.

He was born in Cincinnati, Ohio, December 10, 1834, and was but eighteen years of age when he first saw this valley.

In 1855 he was Corporal in Co. B of the Oregon Volunteers, near Walla Walla where fierce fighting was in progress with the Indians. PeoPeo MoxMox, chief ot the Walla Walla Indians, while attempting a parley with the whites, was taken and held as a hostage. Several other Indians were also held as prisoners. Amos Underwood, a man named Warfield and several others, were acting as guardsmen. The Indians were out in the open, not bound in any way, but were supposed to be without weapons. An order was received from Col. Kelly to send every man to the front. "What shall we do with the Indians?" was asked by one of the guards. "Tie them," was the answer; another voice called out, "Shoot them."

When the guards attempted to tie the Indians, Wolf Skin drew an ugly looking knife, which he had concealed in his clothing, and began striking at the whites. Several shots were fired and a general mixup ensued. In a few minutes four of the Indians were dead, PeoPeo MoxMox being one of the number. It was a time of excitement and confusion and no one knows who was responsible for the death of the Walla Walla chief.

In the latter part of February, 1856, Amos Underwood with three companions, drove a band of stock which had been recovered from the Indians, down to The Dalles. On turning the stock over to the Government, the men received their discharge from service. Mr. Underwood came on down the trail riding his cayuse on his way to the Cascades. As he rode down the mountainside towards Dog River he saw the Joslyn house in flames and knew it was the work of the Indians. He crossed Dog River and went to the home of William Jenkins to pass the night.

Lieutenant Davidson, with a company of soldiers, had come from The Dalles earlier in the day, and when the "Wasco" came in sight on her return from the Cascades, she was hailed and the Lieutenant took his company on board for the purpose of crossing the river and punishing the Indians. Eugene and Charles Coe, Nathan and James Benson, and Amos Underwood accompanied the soldiers. When they approached the north bank of the river they were greeted with yells and saw the trees and rocks alive with redskins. They were greatly outnumbered and without landing came back to the Oregon shore to await further orders. That night a few of the hostile Indians secured boats and crossed over to the south side of the river and attacked the friendly Indians, who fled to the Coe home. The hostile Indians then fired on the guards stationed on the hill above the house but when the guards returned the fire the Indians fled in the darkness. The Jenkins family and all the inhabitants of the settlement spent the night at the Coe home. When morning came the Indians had disappeared. Amos Underwood traveled on to the Cascades and was with the Attwells on the morning of March 26th. He saw the Indians attack the Bradford store and watched them crossing from Bradford Island to the Washington shore.

On August 5, 1859 he filed on a claim at Polalla Illahe, now the site of Ruthton. A little later he located on the North Bank at the place which now bears his name. He married Ellen, an Indian woman, daughter of Chief Chen o wuth. She had a daughter known as Isabel Lear, daughter of Col Lear. This daughter attended school with the white children and received a fair education. Ed Underwood, a younger brother of Amos Underwood, also located on the North Bank and married the daughter, Isabel Lear. They raised a family of eight children, two being pupils in the Barrett School in 1881. Rev. Thomas Condon of The Dalles officiated at the wedding of both Amos and Ed Underwood. Amos Underwood and wife had three children; Jefferson Underwood, born January 28, 1862, died 1878; Mary Underwood born April 17, 1864, John Underwood, born October 23, 1868, died 1882. Mrs. Amos Underwood was highly esteemed by her neighbors as a wise and efficient woman. She died in 1907. Amos Underwood died at his home December 15, 1917, at the age of 83 years. Mary, their daughter, still lives at Underwood.

The following is a copy of a letter written to Putnam Bradford who was visiting in Massachusetts, from Lawrence Coe at the Cascades:

91

"Cascades, W.T., April 6, 1856"

"My dear Put:

"We have had a little tea party since you left, and I will try and give you a little description of the same.

"On Wednesday, March 26, about 8:30 A.M. after the men had gone to their usual work on the bridges of the new railway, mostly on the bridge near Bush's house, the Yakimas came down on us. There was a line of them from the Mill Creek above us to the big point at the head of the falls, firing simultaneously on the men. The first notices were the bullets and the crack of the guns. Of our men, at the first fire, one was killed and several wounded. Will give you a list herein after. Our men, on seeing the Indians, all ran for our store through a shower of bullets, except three who started downstream for the middle blockhouse, distant one and a half miles. Bush and his family also ran into our store, leaving his own house vacant. The Watkins family came to the store, after a Dutch boy, who was lame from a cut in the foot, had been shot in their house. Watkins, Finlay and Bailey were at work on the new warehouse on the island, around which the water was now high enough to run about three feet deep under the bridges.

"There was great confusion in the store at first, and Sinclair, of Walla Walla, going to the railroad door to look out, was shot from the bank above the store and killed instantly. Some of us then commenced getting the guns and rifles which were loaded, from behind the counter. Fortunately about an hour before there had been left with us for transportation below, nine United States Government rifles, with cartridge boxes and ammunition. These saved us. As the upper story of the house was abandoned, Smith, the cook, having come below, and as the stairway was outside where we dare not go, the stovepipe was hauled down, the hole enlarged with axes, and a party of men crawled up, and the upper part of the house was soon secured. We were surprised that the Indians had not rushed into the upper story, as there was nothing or nobody to prevent them. Our men soon got some shots at the Indians on the bank above us. I saw Bush shoot an Indian, the first one killed, who was drawing a bead on Mrs. Watkins as she was running to our store. He dropped instantly.

92

"Alexander and others mounted into the gable under the roof and from there was done most of our firing, it being the best place of observation. In the meantime we were barricading in the store, making portholes and firing when opportunity offered. But the Indians were soon very cautious about exposing themselves. I took charge of the store, Dan Bradford of the second floor, and Alexander of the garret and roof.

"The steamer 'Mary' was lying in the mouth of Mill Creek and the wind blowing hard downstream. When we saw Indians running toward her and heard the shots, we supposed she would be taken, and as she lay just out of our sight and we saw smoke rising from her, concluded she was burning, but what was our glad surprise after awhile to see her put out and run across the river. I will give an account of the attack on her hereafter.

"The Indians now returned in force to us, and we gave everyone a shot who showed himself. They were nearly naked, painted red and had guns, bows and arrows. After a while Finlay came creeping around the lower point of the island toward our house. We shouted to him to lie down behind a rock and he did so. He called that he could not get to the shore, as the bank above was covered with Indians. He saw, while there, Watkins' house burn. The Indians first took out all they wanted—blankets, clothes, guns, etc. By this time the Indians had crossed in canoes to the island, and we saw them coming, as we supposed, after Finlay. We then saw Watkins and Bailey running around—the river side toward the place where Finlay was, and the Indians in full chase after them. As our men came around the point in full view, Bailey was shot through the arm and leg. He continued on, and plunging into the river, swam to the front of our store and came in safely, except for his wounds. He narrowly escaped going over the falls. Finlay also swam across and got in unharmed, which was wonderful, as there was a shower of bullets around them.

"Watkins next came running around the point and we called to him to lie down behind a rock, but before he could do so he was shot in the wrist, the ball going up the arm and out the elbow. He dropped behind a rock just as the pursuing Indians came following around the point, but we gave them so hot a reception from our house that they backed out and left poor Watkins where he lay. We called to Watkins to lie still and we would get him off, but we were not able to do so until after the arrival from The Dalles of the steamer 'Mary' with troops—two days and nights afterwards. During this period Watkins fainted several times from weakness and exposure, the weather being very cold, and he was stripped for swimming, down to his underclothes. When he fainted he would roll down the steep bank into the river, and the ice cold water reviving him, he would crawl back under fire to his retreat behind the rock. Meantime his wife and children were in the store, in full view, and moaning piteously at his terrible situation. He died from exhaustion two days after he was rescued.

"The Indians were now pitching into us right smart. They tried to burn us out; threw rocks and firebrands, hot irons, pitchwood—everything that would burn on to the roof. But you will recollect that for a short distance back the bank inclined toward the house, and we could see and shoot the Indians who appeared there, so they had to throw from such a distance that the largest rocks and bundles of fire did not quite reach us, and what did generally rolled off the roof. Sometimes the roof got on fire and we cut it out, or with cups of brine drawn from pork barrels, put it out, or with long sticks shoved off the balls. The kitchen roof troubled us the most. How they did pepper us with rocks; some of the big ones would shake the house all over. There were now forty men, women and children in the house— four women and eighteen men who could fight, and eighteen wounded men and children. The steamer 'Wasco' was on the Oregon side of the river. We saw her steam up and leave for The Dalles. Shortly after the steamer 'Mary' left. She had to take Attwell's fence rails for wood.

"So passed the day, during which the Indians had burned Iman's two houses, your sawmill and houses, and the lumber yard at the mouth of Mill Creek. At daylight they set fire to your new warehouse on the island, making it as light as day around. I suppose that they reserved this building for the night that we might not get Watkins off. They did not attack us at night, but the second morning commenced as lively as ever. We had no water, but did have about two

94

dozen bottles of ale and a few bottles of whiskey. These gave out during the day. That night a Spokane Indian, who was traveling with Sinclair, and was in the store with us, volunteered to get a pail of water from the river. I consented and he stripped himself nake, jumped out and down the bank, and was back in no time.

"By this time we looked for the steamer from The Dalles, and were greatly disappointed at her non-arrival. We weathered it out during the day, every man keeping his post; never relaxing in vigilance. Every moving object, shadow or suspicious bush on the hill received a shot. The Indians must have thought the house was a bombshell. To our ceaseless vigilance I ascribe our safety. Night came again; saw Shepard's house burn; Bush's house, nearby, was also fired, and kept us in light until about 4 o'clock a.m., when, darkness returning, I sent the Spokane Indian for water from the river, and he filled two barrels. He went to and from like lightning. We, also, slipped poor James Sinclair's body down the slide outside, as the corpse was quite offensive.

"The two steamers now having exceeded the length of time we gave them in which to return from The Dalles, we made up our minds for a long siege and until relief came from below. We could not account for it, but supposed the Ninth Regiment had left The Dalles for Walla Walla, and proceeded too far to return. Morning dawned the third morning, and, lo, the 'Mary' and 'Wasco', blue with soldiers, and towing a flat boat with dragoon horses, hove in sight. Such a haloo as we gave! As the steamers landed the Indians fired twenty or thirty shots into them, but we could not ascertain with any effect. The soldiers as they got ashore could not be restrained, and plunged into the woods in every direction, while the howitzers sent grape after the now-retreating redskins. The soldiers were soon at our store and we, I think I may say, experienced quite a feeling of relief on opening our doors.

"During this time we had not heard from below. A company of dragoons, under Colonel Steptoe, went on down, Dan with them. The blockhouse at the Middle Cascades still held out. Allen's house was burned and every other one below. George W. Johnson's, S.M. Hamilton's, F.A.

Chenowith's, the wharf-boat at Lower Cascades—all went up. Next in order comes the attack on the 'Mary'. She lay in Mill Creek—no fires—and wind hard ashore. Jim Thompson, John Woodard and Jim Hermans were just going up to the boat from our store and nearly reached her as they were fired upon. Hermans asked if they had any guns. No. He went up to Iman's house, the rest staying to get the steamer out. Captain Dan Baughman and Thompson were ashore on the upper side of the creek, hauling on lines, when the fire became so hot that they ran for the woods past Iman's house. The fireman, James Lindsey, was shot through the shoulder. The engineer, Buckminster, shot an Indian on the gang plank with his revolver, and little Johnny Chance, Watkin's stepson, climbing up on the hurricane deck, with an old dragoon pistol, killed his Indian. Johnny was shot through the leg in doing so. Dick Turpin—half crazy, probably—taking the only gun on the steamboat, jumped into a flat boat lying alongside, then jumped overboard and was drowned. Fires were soon under the boiler and steam was raising. About this time Jesse Kemptem—shot while driving an ox team from the sawmill—got on board; also a half-breed named 'Bourbon', who was shot in the body.

After sufficient steam to move was raised, Hardin Cheno-with ran into the pilot house, and lying on the floor, turned the wheel as he was directed from the lower deck. It was almost needless to say that the pilot house was a target for the Indians. After the steamer was backed out and fairly turned around, he did toot that whistle at them good. Toot! Toot! Toot! It was music in our ears. The steamer picked up Hermans on the bank above. Iman's family, Shepard and Vanderpool all got across the river in skiffs, and boarding the 'Mary' went on to The Dalles.

"Colonel George Wright and Ninth Regiment, Second Dragoons, and Third Artillery, had started for Walla Walla and were out five miles, camped. They received news of the attack at 11 o'clock p.m. and by daylight were back at The Dalles. Starting down they only reached Wind Mountain that night, as the 'Mary's' boilers were in bad order because of a new fireman the day before. George Johnson was about to get a boat's crew of Indians, when 'Indian Jack' came running to him saying the Yakimas had attacked the blockhouse. He did not believe it, although he heard the cannon. He went up to the Indian village on the sand bar to get his crew; saw some of the Cascade Indians who said they thought the Yakimas had come, and George now hearing the muskets, ran for home. E.W. Baughman was with him. Bill Murphy had left the blockhouse early for the Indian camp, and had nearly returned before he saw the Indians or was shot at. He returned, two others with him, and ran for George Johnson's, about thirty Indians in chase. After reaching Johnson's, Murphy continued on and gave Hamilton and all below warning, and the families embarked in small boats for Vancouver. The men would have barricaded in the wharf boat but for the want of ammunition. There was considerable government freight in this wharf boat. They stayed about this craft and schooner nearly all day, and until the Indians commenced firing upon them from the zinc house on the bank. They then shoved out. Tommy Price was shot through the leg in getting the boats into the stream. Floating down they met the steamer 'Belle' with Sheridan and forty men, sent up on report of an express carried down by Indian Simpson in the morning. George and those with him went on board the steamer and volunteered to serve under

97

Sheridan. The steamer returned and the Indians pitched into Sheridan; fought him all day and drove him with forty men and ten volunteers to below Hamilton's, notwithstanding he had a small cannon; one soldier was killed.

"The steamer 'Belle' returned next day (third of the attack) and brought ammunition for the blockhouse. Your partner, Bishop, who was in Portland, came up on her. Steamer 'Fashion', with volunteers from Portland, came at the same time. The volunteers remained at the Lower Cascades; Sheridan took his command, and with a batteaux loaded with ammunition crossed to Bradford's Island on the Oregon side, where they found most of the Cascade Indians, they having been advised by George Johnson to go there for the first day of the attack. They were crossing and recrossing all the time and Sheridan made them prisoners. He pressed a boat's crew and as they towed it up to the head of the island and above, saw great numbers of Indians on the Washington Territory side and opposite them. Sheridan expected them to cross and fight him, and between them and the friendly Indians in his charge, he thought he had his hands full. Just then Sheridan discovered Steptoe and his dragoons, infantry and volunteers, coming down from the 'Mary' surprising completely the Indians, who were cooking beef and watching Sheridan across the river. But on sound of the bugle the Indians fled like deer to the woods with the loss of only one killed—'old Joanum'. But for the bugle they ought to have captured fifty.

"So ended the battle. The Ninth Regiment are building a blockhouse on the hill above us; also at George Johnson's, and will hereafter keep a strong force here. Lieutenant Bissel and twelve men who were stationed at the upper Cascades, were ordered away, and left for The Dalles two days before the attack was made upon us. The Indians Sheridan took on the island were closely guarded. Old Chenowith (chief) was brought up before Colonel Wright, tried and sentenced to be hanged. The Cascade Indians, being under treaty, were adjudged guilty of treason in fighting. Chenowith died game; he was hanged on the upper side of Mill Creek. I acted as interpreter. He offered ten horses, two squaws, and a little something to every 'tyee' for his life; said he was afraid of his grave in the ground,

98

and begged to be put in an Indian dead house. He gave a terrific war-whoop while the rope was being put around his neck. I thought he expected the Indians to come and rescue him. The rope did not work well, and while hanging he muttered, 'Wake nike quash copa momaloosa!' He was then shot. I was glad to see the old devil killed, being satisfied that he was at the bottom of all the trouble. But I cannot detail at too great length.

"The next day Tecomcoc and 'Captain Joe' were hanged. 'Captain Joe' said that all the Cascade Indians were in the fight. The next day Tsy, Sim Sasselas and 'Four fingered Johnny' were hanged. The next day Chenoweth Jim, Tunwalth and Old Skein suffered the same fate, and Kenewake sentenced to death, but reprieved on the scaffold. In all, nine were executed. Banaha is a prisoner at Vancouver, and decorated with ball and chain. The rest of the Cascade Indians are on your island and will be shot if they get off from it. Such are Colonel Wright's orders. Dow, Watiquin, Peter, Makooka John and Kotzue, and perhaps more, have gone with the Yakimas.

"I forgot to mention that your house at the lower Cascades, also Bishop's, were burned; also to account for Captain Dan Baughman and Jim Thompson. They put back into the mountains, and at night came down to the river at Vanderpool's place, fished up an old boat and crossed to the Oregon side. They concealed themselves in the rocks on the river bank opposite, where they could watch us, and at night went back into the mountains to sleep. They came in safely after the troops arrived. We do not know how many Indians there were. They attacked the block house, our place, and drove Sheridan all at the same time. We think there were no less than two or three hundred. When the attack was made upon us three of our carpenters made for the middle blockhouse, overtook the cars at the salmon house, cut the mules loose and with the car-drivers all kept on. They were not fired upon until they got to the spring on the railroad, but from there they ran the gauntlet of the bullets and arrows to the fort. Little Jake was killed in the run, and several were wounded. I append a list of the killed and wounded, but this is a long letter; knowing you would be anxious to have all the particulars I have endeavored

99

to give you a true description. Dan is writing to others at home, and he has read this letter. We have got to work again building and transporting; are going to build a sawmill as soon as we can. We had but a few specimens of poor men here during the fight—generally all behaving well. There was, however, one notable exception, a person who arrived at the store a few minutes before the fighting commenced and whose name I will give you in person.

Killed

"George Griswold, shot in leg; B.W. Brown and wife, killed at sawmill, bodies found stripped naked in Mill Creek; Jimmy Watkins, driving team at the mill; Henry Hagar, shot in Watkins' house, body burned; Jake Kyle, German boy, Jacob White, sawyer at the mill; Calderwood, working at the mill; 'Bourbon', half-breed, died on the 'Mary' going to The Dalles; James Sinclair, of the Hudson's Bay Company, Walla Walla; Dick Turpin, colored cook on the steamer 'Mary'; Norman Palmer, driving team at the mill; Three United States soldiers, names unknown; George Watkins, lived four days; Jacob Roush, carpenter, lived six days.

Wounded

"Fletcher Murphy, arm; P. Snooks, boy, leg; J. Lindsay, shoulder; Tommy Price."

Elizabeth Holtgrieve Story Continued

"I was married March 18, 1855, to Henry B. Holtgrieve, who lived down the Columbia River on the Oregon side five miles above Vancouver. We had been married about a year when the Indians attacked the Cascades. Shortly before my sister had come down to stay with my husband and me as she was afraid. She had not been with us two weeks when two steamers, 'The Belle' and the 'Fashion' went up the river on their daily trip. They came back about 2:30 with their flags flying at half mast, and landed at Mr. Lewis Leiser's place, just across the river from our place. He had a

100

woodyard and the steamers landed there for wood. A man named John A. Williams took a boat and went over to see what was the matter. He told us that the Indians had attacked the Cascades, and for everyone on the Oregon side from Sandy River to go to Portland, and those around Cape Horn to go to Vancouver. They went in rowboats. My husband was one who rowed out to warn the people. We were to meet at Mr. Millard's house, two miles below us. When we came to that place everybody was gone and the house locked, so we went to Vancouver.

When my husband returned, he came on down to the Millard house and finding everyone gone, went on down to the ferry. He had his rifle with him and he had to pass an Indian camp. While on the way he heard a boat and tried to hail it but they never answered him. He went up into the attic where he fixed the two dogs on a blanket by an old way sail. In the morning when he woke the sun was already up. He rounded up the cattle and started for the ferry. When he came to the Indian camp he found several women and one man looking up the river. One woman said she was afraid her people were killed. The Indian came up to my husband and asked if he was not afraid. He said 'No.' Then he went on down and met the boats coming back, so Mr. Williams took him in and they went home to get some things they needed. Before they arrived a flatboat landed from the Cascades, on which there was a family named Hamilton and a Mr. Pierce, who had been shot. They had picked everybody along as they came down. They took Mr. Pierce to a hospital, and I think he recovered.

"The next boat was the 'Jennie Clark', from Portland, loaded with volunteers and headed for the Cascades. The next day they came back and landed at Vancouver. The soldiers from The Dalles came down to the Middle Cascades where the Indians were having a barbecue. When the bugle was sounded the Indians ran and took up the trail for Yakima. They had killed several people, amongst them was Mr. Palmer, who had a store at the Middle Cascades. After they killed him, the Indians carried away all of his goods which were later found piled up back in the woods. I never knew what they did with these things.

101

"We did not hear from our folks for about a week, but finally my sister's husband wrote saying they were all alive. He said three men came rushing up warning them that the place had been attacked. My father took his wife and two children in a row boat and crossed the river from Shepard's Point to the Attwell place.

"The river was very rough, the east wind was blowing hard. When they were out in the river they found they had nothing to bail water with, so my stepmother took off her bonnet and bailed the water out of the boat. By the time they arrived on the opposite shore the boat sunk, but they waded out. Just then the steamer 'Mary' came over from the Washington side and took all the women and children to The Dalles. They sawed Mr. Attwell's fence rails for wood to run the boat. They stayed as near the Oregon side as they could, but they were not molested."

The Shepards' land claim of 320 acres later became the site of the town of Stevenson. Their home was on what was called Shepard's Point, on the river's edge behind what is now the Co-Pacific Towboat Company's office.

Thousands of cords of wood were loaded at this point for shipment to The Dalles.

Buried at Stevenson on Shepard's Point are:

Embrusella	1857
Malisia	1863
Lucinda	1889
Richard	

ERASTUS S. JOSLYN AND WIFE OF WHITE SALMON (1853)
D.M.C. Historian

Mr. and Mrs. Joslyn came to White Salmon in the spring of 1853. He was born in Massachusetts on September 17th, 1825, where he grew to manhood and was married to Miss Mary Warner, May 10, 1848.

In 1852 they came to Oregon by way of the Isthmus of Panama, remaining in Portland through the winter. They

102

came to their lonely home in the spring of 1853, locating on the North bank of the Columbia River, the only house east of the Cascades.

In the spring of 1854 Nathaniel Coe, wife and son Henry, made a trip to The Dalles; they were returning on the little steamer "Allen", which became belated and tied up to the North bank to wait for daylight. Mr. Joslyn came to the river and invited the captain, crew and passengers to his home for the night. The invitation was gladly accepted and this was the beginning of a lifelong friendship between the Coe and Joslyn families. The Coe family depended upon the Joslyns for supplies while they were getting established in their new home, and later Sabbath services were held alternately at their homes. When the Indians threatened the Joslyn home they found a temporary refuge with the Coes. When both families had fled to The Dalles for safety, Mrs. Coe and Mrs. Joslyn organized the first Sabbath School ever held there. After the burning of their home in the early days of March 1856, Mr. Joslyn went to The Dalles on business, while Mrs. Joslyn visited with the Attwell family at the Cascades, on the Oregon side. The following letter written by Mrs. Joslyn to a friend at The Dalles and published in the TIMES of March 30, 1881 as a reminiscence, gives a vivid picture of the happenings and struggles of the early pioneers in those days of Indian warfare. She says: "I am very grateful to you for awakening so many reminiscences by your recent postal. I have never saved by writing or picture any one of those early experiences, but they come back to me vividly, freshly as I ponder them o'er, filling my otherwise lonely hours with brighter pictures than I find in books, so that I am only afraid of being too lengthy or egotistical.

"Yes, I was there that March 26th, 1856, waiting at Mr. Attwell's, on the opposite side of the river, while my husband returned to The Dalles on business. You may recollect that only three weeks before I had seen our own home consumed by Indian fires and heard their savage yells as the troops attempted to cross the river, but returned to the Oregon side to await further orders. So, as we heard the firing on the opposite side of the river, and saw the strange course of the steamer 'Mary' as she staggered in the strong current, dropped down, down, turned and trembled and finally made trifling headway upward. We were perhaps more calm than some when the hurrying neighbors said it was the Indians: The woods on the other shore are alive with hostiles; they have killed, will kill everybody; their hideous yells even now come across the water. But see! The Mary' is nearing our shore. We are safe.'

"Mothers hurry their crying children on board; fathers carrying wood and rails, anything to burn, for I think she burned hatchways to get across. We gather a little bedding, a few eatables, but think more of escaping with our lives. At another time we might have said, 'What a bare, comfortless boat', but now it is our only hope. Her every plank meant protection—escape. My first greeting from the engineer was, 'Can you do anything for the wounded?' And as I looked around I realized how narrow the escape—only six men on board; four of them wounded while getting her off; no officer but the engineer. The men who have families on board help as well as landsmen can. We are barely under way when a small boat hails, and a woman is lifted aboard with a babe scarce twenty-four hours old.

"On the bare floor of the little cabin one of the wounded ones is moaning badly, while his life blood is trickling through his blanket and staining the boards. We ask can we help him; try to find him a pillow; but he seems not to understand our language and turns away, so we seek for the others. Little Johnny Chance is in the cook's bunk, crying piteously. 'Where are you hurt, Johnny?' 'Oh, my leg—they will cut off my leg!' And then he cries for his mother. But can we take off his boot and find the bullet in it, having gone clear through the less excited, and he seems to believe us when we tell him, 'They won't cut off your leg.'

"We meet the third man, Jesse, by the engine, holding his shoulder, and trying to show the raw hands how to help, and to our query, 'What can we do for you?' says, 'I am pretty bad, but that fellow in Bush's room is worse." So we go on to find Mr. Lindsay, with the cold drops of perspiration on his forehead, and his lips closely pressed from excessive pain. The ball had passed through his lung. Can we stanch the blood? We find in the engineer's satchel some cotton and make lint as we have read, for not one

104

has had experience. We bathe his hands and face and try to find something to nourish him; succeed in getting a little tea, of which the man in the cabin partakes. The sick woman has a few blankets on the other side of the cabin, and the children are huddled in the corner and the women soothing as best they can, for there is nowhere else to go. As the long hours pass by (the boat runs slowly against wind and current), the engineer is now at his engine, now at the wheel, untiring, calm, masterful. Mrs. Attwell, I think it is, finds us something to eat; some flour on board, and soda that she mixes and bakes while doing her part watching the children and sick. She is a brave, true woman, and I feel ashamed when I see her energy and endurance; but I can't stay long from the sufferer in the little room. To die so! Can we prolong his life until help is reached? We have not time to think of the dear old home so recently devastated as we glide slowly past. The night shadows are gathering now, and weariness and well nigh despair come over me as I steal over the guards and curl down at the end of the boat. Rumor says The Dalles was to be attacked at the same moment with the Cascades. It was just as unprepared, so we may be met by hostile foes instead of our friends. If so, what can we do? No friendly port within reach! We drop back to meet the foe almost anywhere on either side.

"There is no outlet over these impassable mountain ranges. We almost hear savage yells as we round rocky points or steer nearer the shore, to avoid the swift current. It is quite dark now. The man in the cabin has ceased to breathe. Lindsay is sinking. We forget self as we try to minister to his needs. We can give a cup of cold water if nothing more.

"How welcome the cry, 'The Dalles! The Dalles!' The lights are burning as usual. All is well. What a crowd of citizens is on the shore, for word has reached them by the little 'Wasco' of our peril and probable escape. How precious is kindness now. How keenly we appreciate the upper room made ready for us by Mrs. Cushing.

"Lindsay is carried so carefully to a room, and the army surgeon is ready to do all that can be done. After a long illness, he recovered. The engineer has done a grand, brave deed, for which I cannot think he was ever suitably rewarded."

After the immediate danger from the Indians had passed away, Mr. and Mrs. Joslyn went to the Forest Grove neighborhood and lived on a farm for more than a year. In the meantime the Government had built a blockhouse at White Salmon and sub-agent Townsend lived there.

A family by the name of Roberts, missionaries from the South Sea Islands, had located there and when Mr. and Mrs. Joslyn came from their sojourn at Forest Grove they were joined by Mr. Warner and family from Massachusetts. He was a brother of Mrs. Joslyn and took land near them, so that White Salmon was never again the lonely place it had been in former years. Joslyn had business interests in The Dalles, being one of the incorporators of the Wasco Woolen Mills, yet he never lived there more than a few months at a time.

On September 17, 1859, the Congregational Church was organized in The Dalles and Mr. and Mrs. Joslyn were charter members.

More than once Mr. Joslyn represented Skamania County in the Washington Territorial Legislature. In 1875 they sold their home at White Salmon and removed to Colorado Springs, where Mrs. Joslyn died. In 1902 he moved to Santa Barbara, California, and two years later he died at that place, leaving a second wife, formerly Miss Anna Tuck of The Dalles. The FOREST GROVE TIMES says: "Former acquaintances remember him for his hospitality and uprightness of life." H.C. Coe in his writings says: "But I must not forget our dearest friend and kindest neighbor, Erastus S. Joslyn of White Salmon, who had preceded us a year. A man who never let his right hand know what his left did—what we owed him as a neighbor, words cannot tell. Only those who have endured hardships and privations of pioneer life in real earnest can fully comprehend and appreciate such men."

* * * * * * * * * * * * * * * *

Mary Attwell's Story

"We first heard the shooting which carries across the water as if it was much closer, then we saw the steamer 'Mary' coming across the river. Eleanor Joslyn was visiting us and Amos Underwood was with us also. He had seen the Joslyn home burn while coming down the river.

"The 'Mary' needed fuel so they began loading what wood we had and also cedar fence rails. Everyone helped put the fuel aboard. Two rowboats crossed the river, Mr. and Mrs. Shepard with two children and Mr. and Mrs. Felix Iman with two small children in the second boat.

"All aboard we started up the river to The Dalles. The fireman had been badly wounded, shot through the chest. My husband Roger, who had built the boat, was down at Oregon City so was not here to help.

"The inexperienced raw hands, all anxious to help, kept the fire box full of wood but had no idea on how to replace the water in the boiler. When we got about opposite Wind Mountain, the engineer left the engines and came to the fireroom. He found the firebox loaded with fire and the water so low in the boiler that he could not see it in the waterglass. To put water in a dry boiler would have blown us all up. He ordered someone to tell the acting captain to drop anchor, and he ordered the fire pulled and then ran to the engine room and shut the engines down.

"Water was bailed out of the river and thrown into the red hot fire box until the fire was extinguished and when the boiler had cooled enough, the safety valve was unscrewed and water bailed from the river in water buckets was poured down this opening into the boiler. This delayed us what seemed to be a very long time. When the safety valve was screwed into its place the fire was restarted and when the steam pressure was again built up, the engineer then showed the raw hands how to start the steam pump to replace water into the boiler as it was needed.

"The boiler showed damage but we managed to get to The Dalles and found safety."

* * * * * * * * * * * * * * * *

Robert Williams, a Soldier at Fort Rains, tells this Story:

"I was the first person stationed at the blockhouse who suspected that the Indians were preparing for mischief, while carrying a message from Mr. Griswold, who lived at the Middle Cascades, to Mr. Hamilton, who lived on a farm at the Lower Cascades. The word was for Mr. Hamilton to bring up immediately a yoke of oxen which Mr. Griswold had purchased of him, and also to hitch them to one of a lot of new government wagons that were at the landing and bring it up also. Mr. Hamilton started on this mission the next morning, but learned that the Indians were on the warpath. He abandoned the wagon and hastily returned to warn his neighbors and seek safety for himself and family.

"In passing each way by Indian camp, as I had to do, in going to and from carrying the message, my attention was particularly attracted at seeing the majority of the Indians standing together in council and dressed in warlike costumes while some were playing at a game, resembling shinny. Their actions were suspicious and confirmed my belief that they were planning mischief. The movements of some of them in particular, going in a half circle through the timber, thus to flank me, awakened in my mind a very strong suspicion that they were planning to catch me to kill me.

"I did not show to them any evidence that I suspicioned them of doing me harm, but after I got past their camp and out of their sight I hurried with my upmost speed to the blockhouse, and then told Sergeant Kelly and my other comrades my suspicions. But by reason of our belief in the strength of our position, few as they were of us, we did not dread any danger from the Indians, or even think any more about it, for during the whole of the night previous to the attack six out of nine of us there, and an old German, H. Kyle, were drinking whiskey toddy and telling army stories, the old German taking an active part in the sport and claiming to be one of Blucher's Waterloo veterans, but none of them got drunk.

"The next morning the sergeant permitted Frederick to go to the Upper Cascades for a canteen full of whiskey, but unfortunately for him the Indians had commenced their attack on the blockhouse before he returned, preventing him from getting back to us. They shot him through both legs.

He managed, however, to get to the bank of the river, and there hide from sight. He fainted several times from loss of blood, but the whiskey he had in the canteen supported his strength. When night came on he left his hiding place and got safely to the blockhouse, where he received a joyful welcome for we all thought he was killed.

"When the attack first began on the blockhouse, nearly all the men of the detachment were scattered around the vicinity. There were but three of us in close proximity to the blockhouse; Sheridan, and the cook McManus and myself. We all heard the shooting, but strange to affirm, even after the previous, I, nor the two others had even the least suspicion that we were attacked by Indians. My first feeling at such an unusual occurrence was that of indignation at such foolish conduct, thinking all the while that some person was firing off his revolver. But the cook quickly found what was the matter, and immediately gave the alarm, crying, 'Indians!'

"McManus and myself were standing close together near the blockhouse and on the instant the alarm was given we cast our eyes towards the hills and timber which closely surrounded us in front, and then we beheld to our horror the painted and half-naked savages, exultantly firing upon all they could see. McManus who stood by my side was shot in the groin. He died shortly after in the army hospital at Vancouver from its effects.

"I truthfully confess that when I beheld the savages engaged in their bloody work, and my comrade fatally shot, I felt for a few moments as if my hair was lifted from my head. Then my thoughts instantly reverted to the great peril I had escaped the day before, the panoramic view of which will vividly remain stamped on my memory.

"My wounded comrade and myself lost no time in getting inside the blockhouse. I then quickly got on my accouterments and gun, and immediately commenced the defense. The incessant firing and racket of the Indians gave unmistakable warning of deadly danger to those of my comrades who were strolling around. They all got to the blockhouse in safety, excepting Lawrence Rooney, who was so unfortunate as to be captured upon the hill while cutting wood.

"The two or three unfortunate families who were living close by the blockhouse ran to it with all their might for the safety of their lives, but several were severely wounded in running the gauntlet. We had altogether with us, three killed and seven wounded. Among the former was Mr. George Griswold, who might have escaped death but for the confidence in the friendliness of the Indians toward him, and his standing in view and waving to the Indians to cease firing, thinking all the time they were Cascade Indians, whom he well knew, and not suspecting that there was a large force of hostile Yakimas among them.

"The German boy, Jake Kyle, mentioned in Mr. Coe's narrative, was killed while riding on horseback down the road on the hill about 100 yards in front of the blockhouse. The Indian that shot him stood by the side of a tree close to the road, his gun about reaching to the poor boy, who fell instantly upon being shot. It was an agonizing sight to us to behold the poor, unconscious boy writhing in deadly agony for several hours. Sometimes he would endeavor to sit up, but, each attempt provoked the Indians to shoot arrows into him.

"John Switzler and Tom McDowell, and another man to me before unknown, were on their way from the Upper to the Lower Cascades, but before they had proceeded far they discovered hostile Indians. Being unarmed, they made a desperate effort to reach the blockhouse, and providentially did in safety, but greatly fatigued. They proved a valuable acquisition to our small force. The three gallantly aided us during the defense in all duties assigned them to do.

"After they got in, the door was made secure by a bolt and a strong chain. That being completed, we prepared in terrible earnest for our uneven and deadly conflict by giving our savage enemies a treat of canister shot, fourteen rounds in all, from our six-pounder gun which finally made them precipitately retreat for better shelter. We sent after them a few shells for a change. They, however, returned to their first position to pay their respects to us again. But by this time they had learned our mettle, and wisely concluded that they could not whip us, so they returned behind the hill out of range of our guns to torture and put to death our unfortunate comrade, Lawrence Rooney, whom they had captured.

We could not see them at it, but we heard our comrade's piercing screams."

John Attwell later told, "The Indians tied Rooney to a tree and then stuck pitch splinters through his skin and set them on fire." An Indian who was there but did not take part, told this to John a few years later.

"After they had accomplished that last inhuman and diabolical cruelty, the main portion left and went to the lower Cascades. The outrages which they did there are fully narrated in Mr. Coe's narrative. They, however, left enough behind to besiege the blockhouse. But they did not offer to fight us anymore, consequently our little party deemed it advisable to, if possible before night came on, make an effort to get food and water. I volunteered to do so. The sergeant willingly consented to my going. The stranger who joined our force with Switzler and McDowell gallantly volunteered to go with me in search of whatever we could find to sustain life. Our companions in the block-house were meanwhile watching us with guns in hand ready to defend us to the utmost of their ability if occasion offered. But, luckily, we were not molested.

"I went through a window into Mr. Griswold's house, and to my great joy I found a dishpan full of excellent doughnuts. I then handed them to my companion outside to take to the blockhouse, which he did to the delight of all. In the mean-time, I discovered in the pantry a large fine ham, which with the doughnuts, sufficed to relieve all the pangs of hunger. But we failed to get any water. So ended the first day's transaction, but still in constant vigilance by day and night it was necessary to depend for the safety of our lives until we could get assistance.

"The second day, the Indians were still besieging us and thus preventing us from getting elixir, water, which by this time all of us greatly needed, especially the wounded. Close by there was a small saloon, owned and kept by the Palmer brothers, who, with a brother, kept a store at the foot of the hill by the river bank. Luckily they made their escape immediately after the Indians commenced their attack, lock-ing the doors of both of the buildings before they left.

111

"My army comrade, William Houser, suggested that somebody should be allowed to go to the saloon and get whatever they might find that would alleviate hunger and thirst. Sergeant Kelly then permitted him and me to go. The door being locked, my comrade had to break it in with an ax. We procured within one dozen bottles of English porter, one decanter of brandy, the same of whiskey and wine and a small box of oyster crackers. We failed to get water, but the articles mentioned satisfied every requirement except surgical aid.

"We knew relief was close at hand by hearing the report of Phil Sheridan's guns, firing upon the enemy at the Lower Cascades. We relax some of the vigilance we had kept for the purpose of allowing a portion of the guards to take a little rest and sleep. We were greatly fatigued at night during the siege by the service which a vicious bulldog at one

From 1871 Etching

MIDDLE BLOCK HOUSE, CASCADES

112

of the deserted neighbors homes rendered us. He barked and gave warning to us of any attempt the Indians made to get toward the blockhouse. If they had been allowed to get close enough to the building, they would, without doubt, have tried to burn it, by throwing burning pitchwood on the roof.

"The next morning Brevet Lieutenant-Colonel Steptoe, Ninth U.S. Infantry, commanding Companies A.E.F. in all 120 men and officers, came to our relief. The sergeant told them how we had made the defense, and the Colonel then complimented all of us for our admirable conduct."

Had he known...he may not have complimented them on living on English porter and whiskey when river water was only ten feet away from the store where they got the porter...but... they may not have had a container to get water in with them, and the porter was already in a container.

The following is part of Phil Sheridan's Report:

"On the morning of March 26th, the movement began; but the column had only reached Four Mile Creek when the Yakimas, joined by many young warriors—free lancers from other tribes—made a sudden and unexpected attack at the Cascades of the Columbia midway between Vancouver and The Dalles, killed several citizens, women and children, and took possession of the portage by besieging the settlers in their cabins at the Upper Cascades, and those who sought shelter at the Middle Cascades in the old military block-house, which had been built for refuge under just such circumstances. These points held out and were not captured; but the landing at the lower Cascades fell completely into the hands of the savages. Straggling settlers from the lower Cascades made their way down to Fort Vancouver, distant thirty-six miles which they reached that night and communicated the condition of affairs. As the necessity for early relief of the settlers, and the establishment of communication with The Dalles, were apparent, and all the force that could be spared was ordered out; and in consequence, I immediately received directions to go with my detachment of dragoons numbering about forty effective men, to the relief of the middle blockhouse, which really meant to retake the Cascades. I got ready at once, and believing that a piece of artillery would be of service to me, asked for one; but as there proved to be no guns at the post, I should have been obliged to proceed without one had it not been that the regular steamer from San Francisco to Portland was lying at the Vancouver dock, unloading military supplies; and the commander, Captain Dall, supplied me with the steamer's small iron cannon, mounted on a wooden platform which he used in firing salutes at different ports on the arrival and departure of the vessel. Finding at the arsenal a supply of solid shot that would fit the gun, I had it put upon the steamer Belle, employed to carry my command to the scene of operations, and started up the Columbia River at 2 a.m. on the morning of the 27th. We reached the Lower Cascades early in the day, when, selecting a favorable place for the purpose, I disembarked my men and gun on the north bank of the river, so that I could send back the steamboat to bring up any volunteer assistance that in the meantime might have been collected at Vancouver.

"The Columbia River was very high at the time; and the water had backed up into the slough about the foot of the Lower Cascades to such a degree that it left me only a narrow neck of firm ground to advance over towards the point occupied by the Indians. On this neck of land, the hostiles had taken position, and I soon learned by frequent shots, loud shouting and much blustering; then by the most exasperating yells and indecent exhibitions, they dared me to contest.

"After getting well in hand everything connected with my little command, I advanced with five or six men to the edge of a growth of underbrush until we reached the open ground leading over the causeway or narrow neck before mentioned, when the enemy opened fire and killed a soldier near my side by a shot, which just grazing the bridge of my nose, struck him in the neck, opening an artery and breaking the spinal cord. He died instantly. The Indians at once made a rush for the body; but my men in the rear, coming quickly to the rescue, drove them back; and Captain Dall's gun being now brought into play, many solid shot were thrown into

114

the brush where they lay concealed with the effect of considerably moderating their impetuosity. Further skirmishing at long range took place at intervals during the day, with but little gain or loss, however, to either side; for both parties held positions which could be assailed in flank; and only the extreme of rashness in either could prompt a front attack. My left was protected by the river's backwater; and my right rested secure on the mainstream. Between us was the narrow neck of land, to cross which would be certain death. The position of the Indians was almost the counterpart of ours.

"In the evening, I sent a report of the situation back to Vancouver by the steamboat, retaining a large Hudson's Bay bateau which I had brought up with me. Examining this, I found it would carry about twenty men, and made up my mind that early next morning I would cross the command to the other side, south side of the Columbia River, and make my way up along the mountain base until I arrived abreast of the middle blockhouse, which was still closely besieged, and then at some favorable point recross to the north bank to its relief, endeavoring in this manner to pass around and to the rear of the Indians, whose position confronting me was too strong for a direct attack. This plan was hazardous; but I believed it could be successfully carried out if the boat could be taken with me. But, should I not be able to do this, I felt that the object contemplated in sending me out would miserably fail, and the small band cooped up at the blockhouse would soon starve or fall prey to the Indians; so I concluded to risk all the chances the plan involved.

"On the morning of March 28th, the savages were still in my front; and, after giving them some solid shot from Captain Dall's gun, we slipped down the river bank; and the detachment crossed by means of the Hudson's Bay boat, making a landing on the opposite shore at a point where the south channel of the river, after flowing around Bradford's Island, joins the main stream. It was then about nine o'clock; and everything had thus far proceeded favorably. But an examination of the channel showed that it would be impossible to get the boat up the rapids along the mainland, and that success could be assured only by crossing the south channel just below the rapids to the island, along the shore of which there was every probability we could pull the boat through the rocks and swift water until the head of the rapids was reached, from which point to the blockhouse there was smooth water.

"Telling the men of the embarassment in which I found myself, and that, if I could get enough of them to man the boat and pull it up the stream by a rope to the shore, we would cross to the island and make the attempt, all volunteered to go; but as ten men seem sufficient, I selected that number to accompany me. Before starting, however, I deemed it prudent to find out if possible, what was engaging the attention of the Indians, who had not discovered that we had left their front. I therefore climbed up the abrupt mountainside which skirted the water's edge, until I could see across the island. From this point I observed the Indians running horse races and otherwise enjoying themselves behind the line they had held against me the day before. The squaws decked out in gay colors, and men gaudily dressed in war bonnets, made the scene most attractive; but, as everything looked propitious for the dangerous enterprise in hand, I spent little time in watching them; and, quickly returning to the boat, I crossed to the island with my ten men, threw ashore the rope attached to the bow, and commenced the difficult task of pulling her up the rapids. We got along slowly at first; but soon striking a camp of old squaws who had been left on the island for safety and had not gone over to the mainland to see the races, we utilized them to our advantage. With unmistakable threats and signs, we made them not only keep quiet, but also give us much needed assistance in pulling vigorously on the tow-rope of our boat.

"I was laboring under a dreadful strain of mental anxiety during all this time; for, had the Indians discovered what we were about, they could easily have come over to the island in their canoes, and by forcing us to take up our arms to repel their attack, doubtless would have obliged the abandonment of the boat; and that essential adjunct to the final success of my plan would have gone down the rapids. Indeed, under such circumstances, it would have been impossible for ten men to hold out against the two or three hundred Indians; but, the island forming an excellent screen to our movements, we were not discovered; and, when we reached the smooth water at the upper end of the rapids, we quickly crossed over and joined the rest of the men, who in the meantime had worked their way along the shore. We could be very thankful to the old squaws for the assistance they rendered. They worked well under compulsion, and manifested no disposition to strike for higher wages. Indeed, I was so much relieved when we had crossed over from the island and joined the rest of the party, that I mentally thanked the squaws, one and all. I had much difficulty in keeping the men on the main shore from cheering at our success; but hurriedly taking into the bateau all of them it would carry, I sent the balance along the southern bank, opposite the blockhouse. When crossing to the north bank, I landed below the blockhouse some little distance and returned the boat for the balance of the men, who joined me in a few minutes.

"When the Indians attacked the people at the Cascades on the 26th, word was sent to Colonel Wright, who had already gone out from The Dalles a few miles on his expedition to the Spokane Country. He immediately turned his column back; and, soon after I had landed and communicated with the beleagured blockhouse, the advance of his command arrived under Lieut. Col. Edward Steptoe. I reported to Steptoe and related what had occurred during the past thirty-six hours, gave him a description of the festivities that were going on at the Lower Cascades, and also communicated the intelligence that the Yakimas had been joined by the Cascade Indians.

"When the place was first attacked, I also told him it was my belief that when he pushed down the main shore the latter tribe, without doubt, would cross over to the island we had just left, while the former would take to the hills. Steptoe coincided with me in this opinion, and informing me that Lieut. Alexander Piper would join my detachment with a mountain howitzer, directed me to convey the command to the island, and gobble up all who came over to it. Lieutenant Piper and I landed on the island with the first boatload; and after disembarking the howitzer, we fired two or three shots to let the Indians know we had artillery with us, then advanced down the island with the whole command, which had

117

arrived in the meantime. All of the men were deployed as skirmishers, except a small detachment to operate the howitzer. Near the lower end of the island we met, as I had anticipated, the entire body of Cascade Indians, men, women and children, whose homes were in the vicinity of the Cascades.

"They were very much frightened and demoralized at the turn events had taken; for the Yakimas, at the approach of Steptoe, had abandoned them as predicted, and fled to the mountains. The chief and head men put all the blame on the Yakimas and their allies. I did not believe this, however, and to test the truth of their statement, formed them all in line with their muskets in hand. Going up to the first man on the right, I accused him of having engaged in the massacre, but was met by vigorous denial. Putting my forefinger into the muzzle of his gun, I found unmistakable signs of it's having been recently discharged. My finger was black with the stains of burnt powder; and, holding it up to the Indians, he had nothing more to say in the face of such positive evidence of his guilt. A further examination proved that all the guns were in the same condition. Their arms were at once taken possession of; and, leaving a small force to look after the women and children and the very old men, so that there could be no possibility of escape, I arrested thirteen of the principal miscreants, crossed the river to the lower landing and placed them in charge of a strong guard. Late in the evening, the steamboat which I had sent back to Vancouver returned, bringing to my assistance from Vancouver, Capt. Henry D. Wallen's company of the Fourth Infantry and a company of volunteers hastily organized at Portland; but as the Cascades had already been retaken, this reinforcement was too late to participate in the affairs."

The three days' fighting ended, and the army officers caused a thorough search to be made of the surrounding timber. A trail through the woods by which the Klickitats and Yakimas had retreated was followed for ten miles. No Indians were overtaken or captured, though a number were ascertained to have been killed. It being established that the savages had been driven off, Colonel Wright caused to be erected two additional blockhouses, one at the Upper

118

Cascades, and the other near the lower landing and stationed an adequate force at each.

Fort Lugenbeel
Blockhouse built in 1856 at the Upper Cascades

* * * * * * * * * * * * * * * * * *

"I, Mrs. C.S. Corum, was born in Clinton County, Iowa, on the 31st of March 1843, and was the youngest daughter of George and Candace Griswold. In 1851, my father thought it best to try his fortune in the Far West. Our family at that time consisted of my father, mother, three sisters, one brother and myself. My brother and two sisters, not wishing to take the long journey, and having homes of their own, were content to remain where they were. In May my father, mother and their two little girls Gennie and Anna (Eugenia and Christiana) started across the plains. Our team consisted of two yoke of cows and three yoke of oxen and one wagon well filled.

"Here let me say, the cattle were traded off for five horses, and our load lightened by throwing away everything we could get along without before we reached our journey's end. We did not have any trouble with the Indians except stampeding and driving our stock away. One time they drove away all of the stock in the night. I can well remember what fear we held at camp the next day, as nearly all the men went

119

to look for the stock. Father struck their trail, and found them just as the Indians were trying to swim over a river. As he was alone he began shouting and waving his hands for the rest to come on. The Indians thinking the whole train was after them, fled, and he drove the stock back to camp. Another time, as we were preparing to camp, an Indian raised up on the opposite bank and shook a buffalo robe. The team all took fright and ran away. Mother, being out of the wagon, our team ran over, hurting her shoulder, which gave her pain until her death. One man in the train was given to boasting of the good traits of his oxen. He would tell father that if he sang out "Whoa!" to his oxen, they would stop any time at any place. One day he proved it. This man sang out "Whoa!" and his wheel oxen stopped so suddenly that it broke the yoke, and the wagon ran over them. In all of this confusion the man cried out: "There, Griswold, I told you my oxen would stop."

"We did not have hardships and privations in our train like some who were molested, by the Indians, but a trip across the plains in the early days with an oxen team is in itself a hardship enough for one to remember all of one's life.

"We reached The Dalles in October, and went down the Columbia River to the Cascades, where father ran a saw mill that winter. We went to Portland in the spring and stayed until 1854, when we again returned to the Cascades where he resided until his death. If we could have foreseen the terrible tragedies that afterwards took place here, we would have fled the place, but a wise Providence kindly veils our future from our vision, allowing us only to look back on the past scenes of our lives, sometimes with pleasure and sometimes with sad regret.

"Everyone that has read the history of Oregon and Washington is familiar with the terrible deeds done by the Yakima and the Klickitat Indians, and I shall only try to describe a part of the suffering at the Middle Cascades.

"The Cascades was applied to the upper, middle and lower landings of the boats. From the upper landing to the middle was a portage around the falls. The distance two and one-half miles, consisting of a plank railroad and hand cars drawn by mules and horses. From the middle landing to the lower there was a wagon road two and one-half miles. At some stages of the water the steamboats landed at the middle landing, but most of the time bateaux were used. By those means all of the government and individual ammunition and freight was transported around the falls.

Father's occupation was transporting the freight. Captain Wallen, with the assistance of father's work hands and mule teams had made a blockhouse near our house, and several nights we stayed in it when the Indian excitement ran high. I have passed briefly over my life up to this time, as nothing transpired to mar the happiness of my childhood. But soon, ah! very soon, I was to take part in scares that can never be obliterated from my memory.

On the 26th day of March 1856, the sun rose over a happy prosperous little village at the middle landing, but ere it reached its mid-day course, death and devastation reigned in our midst. As we were living in a place I shall try and describe some of the suffering here. Between the hours of 8 and 9 o'clock in the morning, when everyone was busy at their different occupations, the Indians attacked these three landings at the same time. At the lower landing the settlers were warned by a half-breed Indian, and all got into a boat and started down the Columbia River without any loss of life, and some only slightly wounded. The Indians burned everything that was left. At the upper landing they killed several, wounding some also. By all collecting at Bradford's store they held the place with great difficulty until help came from The Dalles. Here everything was burned. The blockhouse was situated on the bank of the Columbia River and was open to an attack on one side only. From this point the Indians began firing. Thinking it was the soldiers firing off their guns, as they sometimes did, I walked out in the yard and stood talking to some others. Six bullets in rapid succession came over my head and about me, the last one striking a little boy by my side. He cried out, "I am shot!" Then we seemed to understand that we were in danger and went in the blockhouse. By this time people in every direction came flying in. They had taken all the soldiers to The Dalles, but seven, and one of these was lying dead upon the hill in front of the blockhouse and another one shot through the hip at the foot of the incline where they hauled the freight up, leaving five, with the assistance of the settlers, to fire the cannon and hold the fort. Mother was going to the spring for water and came in with the bucket on her arm. Several came in wounded, but only one fatally, which was my father. He was shot in the knee while some distance from the fort, but reached it in time to sink down inside the door. On seeing me first he said, "Is mother here?" I supported his head in my arms while mother took a black handkerchief from his neck, and also some of her clothing, and tried to stop the flow of blood, but alas! too late to save him. With the cannon booming over his head, he sank quietly to rest.

> Calm the good man meets his fate,
> Guards celestial around him wait.

Everyone was at their post and the yells of savages and the cannon's roar was kept up all during the day. For two days and nights mother and I sat on either side of our dead, and now, as I recall the scenes of those sad days spent in the blockhouse tears dim my eyes.

"Often, before his death, father tried to persuade mother to take me (my sister being in Portland attending school), and go to Portland. She would tell him if he stayed, she would also. He said he was needed here, and he could not leave. Alas! for the brave man who would desert his post. Alas, for his widow and orphan children. A pitiful sight indeed, it was to see a German boy, who was shot down in sight of the fort, as he would raise his hand and beckon to the fort, the Indians seemed delighted in his suffering, and would shoot him with arrows to increase his pain. He died the first night and lay in sight of the fort until the third day. The Indians had piled cord wood on the soldier they had killed on the hill, it was supposed with the intention of burning him, but for some reason they did not. The one, who was wounded on the incline, crawled up the bank the first night and came into the blockhouse. The second night towards morning, the Indians ceased firing, and the third day they drew off to re-enforce the upper and lower landings. They were seen crossing the river below the fort, and immediately the cannon was fired, but they were too far away. What a welcome sound was the booming of this cannon, for it seemed that therein lay our safety. Although it has been quite a number of years since I heard the firing of those guns, yet now, when I hear the report of a gun ring out on the night air, my thoughts fly back to those nights of peril.

"All of this time we were without food of any kind or a drop of water. The soldier's kitchen was apart from the blockhouse, and during the firing no one dared to venture out. The third day soldiers came from The Dalles and volunteers from Portland and we were liberated. The greatest excitement prevailed, as the friendly Indians had joined the hostile band. Every family was leaving the fort. Tenderly laying our loved ones to rest, we bade him a long farewell and went to Portland. What sad news to convey to that sister—our father dead, and home and property damaged. A flatboat loaded with 250 bushels of potatoes (at that time worth $2.00 a bushel) turned loose on the Columbia River, and as we floated down, it seemed to me we were friendless indeed.

I must speak of some others that, like myself, saw the bullets fall thick around them. One man by the name of Murphy came riding over the hill on one of the horses cut loose from the cars. His brother Jim, coming on down the railroad, and saw the horse fall with him, as it was shot in the neck. He started to go for him, but he cried out for him to go back. Jim stood until his brother came up to him and they went in the fort together. Jim escaped unharmed, but the other was severely wounded in the shoulder. These men came down on the railroad and as they neared the fort the bullets became thicker and thicker. One man said, "See Jim run." And at the same time a bullet struck him in the shoulder. He being the last one, and there was not room for one man to pass another on the railroad, he cried out to the one in front of him: "Run, Peter, run." Peter, who was a German, answered, "I can run no faster." "Well, then, let me run," said Jim, and he stepped aside and Jim passed him, and all reached the fort safely.

"A few years after this time, the fort and the bank on which it stood slipped into the river, but the safety it gave to the people at that massacre will never be forgotten. We reached Portland on my thirteenth birthday—31st of March.

123

I was placed in school with my sisters at the ladies seminary. The following June my mother returned to the Cascades to settle up the estate, but there was not much left for us. (I am at this time trying to have my Indian depredation claims settled.)

"My sister was married in 1858 and died in 1863, leaving two boys. Mother died in 1877 in Prineville, Oregon. Myself, one brother, and one sister, who is in Iowa, are all that is left of the family that parted on the banks of the Mississippi in 1851. Ah, such is life.

"I was married in the year 1860, and am the mother of six children. I have tried to write as explicit as possible, and will be pleased to see my father's and mother's name rank with the brave-hearted, noble suffering and enduring first pioneers of the Cascades area on the mighty Columbia River."

* * * * * * * * * * *

Joseph Bailey crossed the plains in 1853 and settled at the Cascades. He joined the volunteer army in 1855 to help control the hostile Indians east of The Dalles and was on duty at Fort Dalles when the Indians attacked the Cascades. In 1862 he helped rebuild the Washington portage for the steam locomotive. In 1863 he was placed in charge of the Eagle Creek sawmill. Among his employees at the mill was John Stevenson, a pioneer who had homesteaded at Cape Horn in 1853. John's sister was hired as cook for the mill's cookhouse. She was a widow with three small children and such a splendid cook that the mill superintendent fell in love with her, and on January 24, 1864 she became Mrs. Bailey, and Joe a father of three kids.

* * * * * * * * * * *

Early, Well-Liked Indian Agent
James Harvey Wilbur was born September 11, 1811, in New York State. When he reached 20 years of age he married Lucretia Ann Setphens on March 9, 1831.

Wilbur was a giant of a man not only physically but religiously. He was tall, broad-shouldered and carried more than 300 pounds of brawn and muscle. He was a Methodist and preached the religion where he could. He worked some as a policeman in New York and never carried a gun. Once two hoodlums attacked him and he grabbed each by the nape of the neck and cracked their heads together so hard they both ended up in the hospital.

When George Gray was sent to head the Oregon Mission in the new western territory, he chose Wilbur to follow him to Oregon.

The Wilburs sailed from New York in September 1846, southward around Cape Horn of South America. The sailing ship, "Lausanne" needed painting and Wilbur volunteered to help with this work while on the long slow journey. Nine months at sea was too much to sit idly by, so he was lowered over the side of the ship in a bos'n basket with his paint pail and brush. This day the seas were quite rough and the basket let go into the sea, painter, paint and all.

Shouts aroused Captain Gelstonwas, "Man over board!" Sails were furled and a lifeboat let overboard and the sailors battled the rough seas to reach him. He was brought back to the ship and then on board he clasped his weeping wife and daughter and thanked the captain for picking him up. He was soon hanging over the side finishing his painting but with a stronger rope. The little ship reached the Columbia and crossed safely over the bar and up to the Willamette River. They went ashore in Oregon, June 27, 1847.

Oregon extended from California to British Columbia and from the Pacific to the Rocky Mountains. This was to be his working area.

He chose a place in Douglas County for his first headquarters. The place later became called Wilbur. He was instrumental in founding several educational institutions, among them Umqua Academy.

Rev. Wilbur on his many trips up the Columbia met with Nathan Olney of The Dalles, and a great friendship developed. He became well liked by the Indians wherever he went. The Indians about the Cascades called him "Siwash Tyee"—Indian Boss. He had been appointed sub-Indian Agent by Mr. Palmer. White people and the Indians both loved the new agent. Indians knew that he was firm and fair and they came to trust him, they felt that he was like a father to them, so they started calling him Father Wilbur and he came to be called that by the whites as well.

He often stopped to visit the Joslyns at Bingen, the Olneys at The Dalles or the Attwells at Cascade Falls. The Attwells named their second son John Wilbur Attwell after James Wilbur.

Indian Chief Skaminah back of Grand Dalles (now called Dalles Port) on the north bank of the river, was stirring up the Indians into hostile acts. Father Wilbur went to this tribe with the sheriff to see what could be done to quiet them. Skaminah would not listen to the sheriff so he attempted to arrest Skaminah. The Indians became hostile until Wilbur, six feet four inches tall, broad-shouldered, and weighing over 300 pounds, reached over and took the chief by the hair and started for the Grand Dalles with him in tow. When the sheriff and Wilbur with the chief reached the boat to cross the river to The Dalles the chief wouldn't get into the boat, Wilbur picked him up and planted him in the boat. When they reached The Dalles the chief wouldn't leave the boat until he saw Wilbur reaching for his hair, then he willingly came along. He was brought before the judge at The Dalles and soon agreed that it was best to remain peaceful and keep his tribe peaceful also. Wilbur took him back across the river and back to his tribe. Chief Skaminah then became one of the best "injuns" on the river. He remained peaceful and became well liked by the settlers. When the new county was made the oldtimers said the county was named after this Chief, but slightly mispelled into Skamania. This chief's tribe was in the center of the new county.

The military campaigns of Wright, Steptoe and Garnett had left the Indians crushed. The Yakimas had been deserted by their Chief Kamaikan who had led them into the war with the whites. Father Wilbur's heart bled for these crushed people of a proud nation. He went to them and preached God to them and won their confidence; they saw in him a white man with no "forked tongue".

Wilbur rode a large mule where ever he went. No horse could carry over 300 pounds along with saddle and camping equipment so he always rode this large mule. He got Snipes, who owned many cattle in the area, to help with the Indians. Snipes gave them some cattle to start their own herds with.

Whenever Wilbur's duties would allow him spare time, he would get aboard the big mule and ride down to The Dalles and visit with Nathan Olney. Wilbur urged Nathan to give up his ferry across the Columbia and to join him at Fort Simcoe. Nathan had been shot by an Indian with an arrow some time before and it was slow healing.

The agent over Wilbur was not honest with the Indians and Wilbur pleaded with the agent to treat the Indians fairly and honestly. The agent fired Wilbur and ordered him off the Reservation. His wife was teaching the Indians there at the tme.

Father Wilbur was not one to take injustices meekly. He headed for Washington, D.C. Crossing the Rocky Mountains in the dead of winter, battling snow and blizzards along the way. Arriving, he sought and was granted an audience with President Lincoln. The President upon looking at Wilbur and studying his weathered face and listening to his story, was impressed with this man's character and sincerity and he asked him many questions about the future relationship with the Indians, and how better to build up feelings between the races. President Lincoln commissioned Rev. James Wilbur, Agent for Fort Simcoe to replace the present agent as soon as he could return to the fort.

The Indians were pleased to see Father Wilbur return and be in charge and the friendship lasted for 20 years until he retired, in 1882. His friend Olney joined him at the work but fell from his horse and was killed, and buried at Fort Simcoe.

Letters Received by the Topographical Bureau of the War Department, 1826-1865

San Francisco, April 4, 1856

Major:

I am authentically informed that the Cascades W.T. is now in possession of a hostile Indian force which has burned

127

the buildings and driven off the settlers of that vicinity. A blockhouse erected by Maj. Rains is still standing, and its garrison at last accounts was defending their lives from the attack of an overwhelming force of savages. As I wish to commence operations on the road at the Cascades immediately after the Spring rains have ceased, which will probably be early in the month of May, this information is of considerable moment. If the savages are to remain in possession of the Cascades the work would be delayed and even if driven off, it will be difficult to procure laborers to go up there unless their safety is in some way assured.

I have therefore respectfully to call your attention to this state of affairs and to request that you will make a requisition for a sufficient Guard properly officered, to preserve quiet at the Cascades during the progress of the work.

With high respects,
Your obt. svt.
George H. Derby
1st Lt. Topl. Engineers

Maj. Hartman Bache
Superintendent Military Roads

* * * * * * * * * * *

San Francisco, Cal., April 5th, 1856
Brig. Genl. John E. Wool, Br. Maj. Genl.
Com'g. Department of the Pacific
Sir:

In endorsing the opinion of the necessity of a guard to protect the workmen against the Indians in the operations about to commence at the Cascades under the act of the 6th of February 1855 "for the continuation of a Military road from the Dalles of the Columbia to Columbia City Barracks" expressed in the letters of 1st Lieut. Derby, Topogl. Enge. dated yesterday of which the enclosed is a copy, I beg leave to state that it was the intention of the Hon. the Secretary of War before I left Washington, to give me authority to call on the General commending the Department subject of course to his discretion, for guard in case they became necessary to carry out the object of the laws in regard to Military roads generally on the Pacific Coast.

I have the honor to be, Sir,
Very Respectfully,
Your obt. Sevt.
Hartman Mache
Maj. Topogl. Enge. B. Maj.

* * * * * * * * * * * *

Bache enclosure of May 8 (sic), 1856. George Derby to Maj. Bache, May 13 (sic), 1856, Portland, O.T. (First portion of letter concerns other portions of the Military Road)

....I find that during the winter parties of volunteers have explored the South side of the Columbia, opposite the old Portage and finding the country favourable have constructed a rough road which already bids fair to remove the travel entirely to that side of the river. It is represented to me by good authority that this road is susceptible of being made a perfectly level & excellent route at far less cost than that of the line surveyed by me, that the landings are better & more easily made & that for the whole distance the route runs over a level rocky plateau where nothing will be required but the construction of culverts, ditches, and one or two small bridges to put it in a better condition than the other side could be made, for the rock being loose rock & gravel, it may be macadamized, and no planking be necessary.

If then on careful examination I find these statements to be facts, and that a good road can be made on the South bank at considerably less cost than on the North bank, all these things being equal, I suppose it will be my duty to perform the task accordingly.

Of course this change of plans requires your authority, but I know twenty-five men here who have paid their own expenses to this place to obtain employment & I feel compelled to go to work immediately. If I were to wait until I could hear from you the government would be put to a large & useless expenditure, and I shall therefore go to work at once on the South bank if I become satisfied that it is for the interest of the Government to have the road made on that bank....

It may be considered that I am greatly to blame for not having surveyed the South bank last season and ascertained these facts myself. But at the time I made my survey there were no persons to be found who knew anything in favor of that side, those who had been there represented the country rugged rocky broken up by ravines, there was no trail, & the rocks certainly presented a most repelling aspect. On the other bank, a tolerable road existed for a great part of the way, and it seemed proper & more economical to take advantage of that circumstance, a survey of the South bank would have been very expensive, & I thought it useless to attempt it. It is probable that it was an error in judgment and I certainly regret not having made a reconnaisance of that side of the river. If I had done this, as no improvements had then been made however, it might still have appeared that the North bank presented the most favorable route.

The road partially constructed by private enterprise will probably now throw the balance in favor of the South bank...

It is possible that the advantage of the South bank route may have been exaggerated to me by interested individuals. I think not however, as much of my information is from the Quarter Master to the officers stationed at Vancouver.

Of course I shall do no work on that route until thoroughly satisfied by personal examination that it is the best...

* * * * * * * * * * * *

Derby to Bache, 14 May 1856, Portland

....It appears that the statements in my first letter are facts so far as regards the road made by the Volunteers but that this road is but two miles in length, that at present steamboats can land at its terminus, but when the River is high they cannot, & that to make a road from that point to a landing that may be used at all times, a steep and rocky hill has to be cut down, and a bridge some 300 feet in length to be built. These operations it is said will cost far more than those constructed on the North side.

I shall therefore encamp my party at the usual landing on the North Bank and then proceed to examine carefully the proposed route upon the South bank...

* * * * * * * * * * * *

Bache to Derby, May 19, 1856, San Francisco, California.

....employment of (Daniel) Wright for the road at the Cascades of the Vancouver & Dalles Military Road...in my opinion judicious. I may promise in regard to the occupation of the South side of the river at the Cascades by the contemplated road that I cannot realize, considering the difficulties which have always attended the passage of this obstruction, it should only now appear that the ground is more favorable than on the North side. If, however, it should so turn out, and require a road no longer or at least not much longer than the one in the north line of the river, you are hereby authorized to make the road on the South side. An objection to this course would at first view seem to conflict with the law which makes the appropriation for a road in Washington Territory...

* * * * * * * * * * * *

Camp "Bache" Cascades W.T.

May 19, 1856

Major:

On arriving at the Cascades I proceeded to explore the South Bank of the river in company with Mr. Wright.

We found a tolerable road had been made on that side, extending from a point nearly opposite to the upper landing some two miles down the river, to a landing place called Ruckels. Steam Boats cannot get up to this landing, but goods intended for transportation on the South bank are landed at a point opposite the lower landing on the N bank (Johnson's) and then carried up in bateaux.

This course cannot be pursued at all stages of the river and to make a good route on the South bank it would be necessary after improving the road already made, to continue it down the river nearly three miles to the landing place opposite Johnson's. Two miles of this road might be made at ordinary expense, but a long expensive bridge would be required across a creek about a mile below Ruckel's. There the last mile presents great difficulties to be encountered, and one obstacle which appeared to us on examination nearly impassable. This is an immense rock rising precipitously from the bank of the river to a height of 120 feet from whose summit rises a rugged and inaccessible mountain. A pack trail leads over the summit of the rock, but the ascent is too steep to admit of the construction of a wagon road.

This rock is called "the Tooth." The only feasible plan for passing it is to build a bridge around it, some 400 feet in length, which would be very expensive and would be constantly liable to be washed away or destroyed by drifting timber. We concluded after a careful examination of the localities that a road on the South bank would be more expensive than that on the North Bank and accordingly returned to the other side and commenced operations. The soil on the L. Bank is however the best; it is gravelly and with plenty of loose crumbling rock interspersed and were a road made on that side it would not require planking. Still I believe it would cost more to make a road around "the Tooth" than to plank the other road clear through—my party consisting of twenty six laborers, under Mr. Wright are now encamped in a field belonging to Mr. Chenowith, somewhat over a mile from Johnson's Landing. We are now engaged in cutting and clearing a new road on each side of the Creek for approaches to a bridge, on which I have a force engaged that will finish it by the end of this month. The mules, casks, wagons, and all other materials are on the grounds and all should go on well. The Military force at this place has been reduced one half, there being now but fifty men stationed here. A dread of the Indians is still felt here, and no soldier is allowed to leave his quarters unarmed, and an order has been issued that officers riding across the Portage shall take with him an escort of five men. Howbeit, we encamped in an isolated position unarmed and unprotected and remained undisturbed for three nights when yielding to the representations of the officers and others I made a requisition of the Ordinance officers at Vancouver for arms & ammunition and receiving them, armed some of my laborers and put them on guard at night.   The Irishmen who had been very comfortable and serene before took these warlike preparations to be an admission on my part that there was some danger, and the next morning two of them refused to work without receiving higher wages.   Of course I ordered them out of Camp, and they held out half a day, when they returned, and expressing their sorrow were allowed to go to work again, after I had made them an harangue which appeared to produce a good effect.

It is very difficult to procure (men?).   The prices paid ($50 per month) seems very high but I have had very few applications from labouring men of the country, and none that I would accept of late.   Nearly all the men employed on this work are from San Francisco.   Things look well here at present.   In my monthly report I shall give you a full account of the work.

* * * * * * * * * * *

The Indian trouble and attack on the north bank of the river put Bradford's Company out of business.   The company was not long recovering.   The stern-wheel steamer "Hassalo", tonnage 581 and 181 feet long was built at the Attwell boat yard, to replace the "Mary".   The "Senorita", a side-wheeler built at Oregon City was purchased to replace the "Belle".

The Ruckel's "Transportation Company" met this new competition by building the side-wheeler "Mountain Buck" at Portland; she was 133 feet long.   They also started building a railroad, similar to the one across the river. They leased the right-of-way from John Chipman for $50 per year.

As competition grew the two companies agreed, "If you can't lick 'em, join 'em," so they combined as the UNION TRANSPORTATION LINE.   With the new setup the Oregon Portage was closed and the "Wasco" and "Senorita" taken off the runs.   This agreement did not last, so within a year the Oregon Portage was back in operation.

133

A mill was built at Eagle Creek and men were employed to build a railroad on the south bank. The railroad was constructed of wood. The rails were of 6-inch square timbers, covered with strap iron and laid at a gauge of five foot. Between the rails was a plank walk for the mules. The railway was operating in early 1859. It had one covered passenger car and several freight cars, which were small and all 4-wheelers.

Bradford and Ainsworth worked through Ben Stark. Bradford went along with the deal, hoping to curb the Ruckel portage from encroaching upon the business of the older portage.

Competition was again strong so the two rivals joined in a new agreement. The new company was again called the "Union Transportation Company". On May 12, 1860 this company then incorporated under the name "Oregon Steam Navigation Company". Ladd & Tilton money and Ainsworth were now in the company. Colonel Ruckel was director of the new company and Dan Bradford, vice-president.

The Bradford Portage shut down in May 1861 and the Oregon portage took over all business. John Chipman deeded his donation land claim to Olmstead Aug. 31 for $11,000. John Tanner at Tanner Creek sold his land claim to Olmstead November 15th. The Oregon Portage purchased a small locomotive from the Vulcan Iron Works in San Francisco. A barge was built to serve as a wharf boat at the lower landing. The little locomotive arrived on the ship "Pacific" and it was loaded on the barge and towed up the river to the portage. Five steam boats assisted in towing the barge and 'locie' into the swift water at the landing; the "Carrie Ladd", the "Julia", the "Mountain Buck", the "Rival" and the "Independence". The little 0-4-0 locomotive was named the PONY and placed on the rails. This was the first steam locomotive in the northwest.

The iron works had sent Mr. Goffe along to show the new owners how to run it and when Ruckel saw how the little fellow loved the PONY, he hired him to be the engineer.

When steam was raised, Col. Ruckel, W.S. Ladd, R.R. Tompson, S.G. Reed, Capt. Gilman, Put Bradford and John Scranton crawled aboard for the first ride. There were no cars hooked to the PONY so they all stood in the tender. The PONY belched out smoke, and cinders mixed with steam which soon covered the well dressed passengers until their plug hats and stiff white shirts appeared as if they had crawled from the gutter.

The new side-wheel steamer the "Idaho" of 278 tonnage and 147 feet long had just been built at the Attwell boat yard and was waiting to take the dirty dignitaries aboard.

When the little PONY started on her return to Bonneville a crowd of 300 Indians lined the side of the track. Goffe blew the whistle and the chief rushed alongside and called out, "Hi you skookum, Siwash," (Big strong chief). Mr. Goffe invited him aboard and he enjoyed the ride so much he became a nuisance, wanting to ride every trip.

The PONY pulled an average of 200 tons of freight each day over the portage, for one year.

The Washington people at the Cascades with pressure on the Washington Legislature, secured a charter to build a steam railroad on the north bank. Bradford and Company soon became owners of this charter and sold it to the O.S.N. Co. along with their road bed and mule powered equipment. Ainsworth became president of the new company, and by 1863 the Washington portage was rebuilt and in operation. Finer boats were put into service, freight decks below with fine cabins above, the cabins opened with a "Ladies Saloon" forward, to which the delicate might retire and be away from tobacco and cigar smoke. The boats were larger and faster and grander. Large glass chandeliers hanging from the ceiling of the dining room.

All traffic must go around the Cascades via this portage. The O.S.N. controlled the transportation and set their own prices. In 1861 the company carried 10,500 passengers around the Cascades and 6,290 tons of freight; by 1864, 36,000 passengers and 21,834 tons of freight went over the portage.

Many stories have been passed down on the procedures of making freight rates, charges were made by measure as well as weight. Forty cubic feet was a ton regardless of weight, constituted a ton of shipping charges. Measuring the cubic content of a farm wagon was made by measuring its width, its length with tongue extended and its height by raising the tongue straight up.

Cascade City (now known as North Bonneville) was then the largest city in Washington Territory, larger than Seattle or Tacoma.

Leaving Portland one boarded the steamer at 4 or 5 in the A.M., had breakfast on board for 25¢ and arrived at the Lower Cascades around 11 A.M. The passengers walked ashore to the portage passenger car while the freight was wheeled aboard the train.

The first locomotive on the north bank portage was a 4-1-0 which indicated it only had one driver wheel on each side. Then the whistle blew and the train moved the six miles to the upper landing. This meant another long wait while the freight was unloaded from the train onto the second boat. Many walked over to the Bush Hotel for lunch or a drink as he also operated a saloon and a hospital. The loaded boat blew the whistle and the passengers went aboard. Arriving at The Dalles you had your choice of two hotels, the Cosmopolitan or the Umatilla House. If you were lucky enough to find a room, you might need to share it with a stranger, 123 rooms and 2 baths.

The gauge of this railroad was changed 3 times, from 5 feet to 4 feet 8-1/2 inches, and then later to narrow gauge of 3 feet.

The little PONY was shipped to The Dalles in 1863 to be used on the Celilo Portage, but after remaining there 3 years it was sold to David Hewes for $2,000. It was then taken to San Francisco, where it was used hauling sand in construction work. Years later Mr. Hewes stored it in a warehouse for 20 years. The building burned and the PONY became a "skeleton". Henry Dosch discovered the little locie and told Col. Hawkins of the find and it was rebuilt and taken to the 1905 Lewis & Clark World's Fair in Portland. After the Fair it ended up at the Union Depot in Portland. Mr. Wayne Gurley and a few others managed to get the little locomotive moved to its permanent home near the old locks at Cascade Locks, Oregon, where it can be seen and touched.

Assessment and Statistical Roll
Skamania County — Year A.D. 1860

Name of Persons	Pole Tax
1. John McClellon	1.00
2. John D. Woodward	1.00
3. E.C. Hardy	1.00
4. James L. Furgeson	1.00
5. C.J. Palmer	1.00
6. Jake Givens	1.00
7. Flos Givens	1.00
8. E.W. Reynolds	1.00
9. E.W. Baughman	1.00
10. George W. Johnson	1.00
11. Geo. H. Knaggs	1.00
12. A.W. Grenzeback	1.00
13. James Murphy	1.00
14. Pat McCarty	1.00
15. James Wilson	1.00
16. Pat Galleger	1.00
17. E. Merida	1.00

18.	P.C. Dennis	$1.00
19.	L. L. Barnes	1.00
20.	J. Sorenson	1.00
21.	E. Sutheiran	1.00
22.	Thos. Reynolds	1.00
23.	Geo. W. Murray	1.00
24.	A. G. Bradford	1.00
25.	F. G. Iman	1.00
26.	John Willis	1.00
27.	John Troles	1.00
28.	H. Corum	1.00
29.	M. Coyne	1.00
30.	W. W. Markwell	1.00
31.	James Hilligas	1.00
32.	Levi Fields	1.00
33.	Henry Shepherd	1.00
34.	J. M. Findley	1.00
35.	James Lindsey	1.00
36.	Geo. Fields	1.00
37.	James Murphy	1.00
38.	Fletcher Murphy	1.00
39.	Wm. M. Murphy	1.00
40.	Joseph Robbins	1.00
41.	Elizabeth Snooks	1.00
42.	G. P. Roberts	1.00
43.	Wm. Benson	1.00
44.	Wm. O. Brigham	1.00
45.	E. S. Joslyn	1.00
46.	W. B. Stillwell	1.00
47.	Arthur Kincella	1.00
48.	John W. Stephenson	1.00
49.	John M. Stephenson	1.00
50.	R. C. McWilliams	1.00
51.	Isaac H. Bush	1.00
52.	John Donoran	1.00
53.	P. Leonberg	1.00
54.	D.C. Pomroy	1.00
55.	Geo. Mitchell	1.00
56.	Thos. Brown	1.00
57.	Eranville Plemmins	1.00
58.	Simeon Gile	

59. Thomas Monaghan	$1.00
60. Saul Baughman	1.00
61. Wm. Wilson	1.00
62. Thos. Wilson	1.00
63. John Whitmore	1.00
64. John Cowen	1.00
65. S.M. Hamilton	1.00
66. John Johnson	1.00
67. D.H. Ferguson	1.00
68. Lewis Hart	
69. Thos. McNatt	
70. J.K. Bailey	1.00
71. A. Jacobs	1.00
72. P.F. Bradford	1.00
73. D.F. Bradford	1.00
76. Dusia Gallentine	1.00
77. Chas. Blissett	1.00

The above information is as near correct and as much information as I can obtain from the addressors and census taken and returned. We have no schools and no churches. I believe all the farms have fruit trees.

Total value of property assessed in Skamania County amounts to $66,636.00.

Respectfully,

E.W. Reynolds

Mr. E.C. Hardy will send you a copy of the census and Absentee Roll. I have done an immense amount of work for nothing and intend to resign my office immediately!

* * * * * * * * * * *

Hood River Historical Society File

Mary Underwood Lane was born April 17, 1864 in N. Bonneville, Wn.—then known as Chief Wa-bana-ha's Village. Her parents were Amos and Ellen (Chen-o-Wuth Lear) Underwood.

Amos Underwood, born in Cincinnati, Ohio in 1838, came to Oregon country from Missouri in 1852. A private in the Yakima wars 1855, a corporal later in the Oregon Volunteers. He gave up soldiering and in 1859 purchased the pre-emption claim of Peter Rudio. This is at present the Morton Ranch at Ruthton in Hood River County. After selling this claim he moved to Skamania County, Wn. and homesteaded, using his soldier's warrant.

Mary Lane's mother, Ellen Chen-o-Wuth, daughter of Chief Chen-o-Wuth of the Cascade Indians, was first married to Lt. William King Lear in 1856. One year after the birth of a daughter Isabella, Ellen & Lt. Lear separated and in 1861 Ellen Lear married Amos Underwood by Indian rights.

She was known as Aunt Mary to the entire Mid-Columbia area. A life member of the Sons & Daughters of Pioneers & a charter member of Hood River Historical Society.

*It will be noticed that Chief Chen-o-Wuth was later mispronounced as Chenoweth by the whites.

Settlements called "Cascades" Confusing

The first emigrants called the rapids, the Cascades. The portage around the cascades on the north bank, used the names Lower Cascades, Middle Cascades and Upper Cascades for its three terminals. When the portage was improved with 6 miles of railroad the little city of Cascades City near the lower landing becoming the most populated town in Washington Territory, much larger than Tacoma or Seattle. The Upper Cascades then became known as Bradford's Landing.

Across the river on the south bank, the lower landing of Ruckel's portage was called Lower Cascades Oregon Side;

141

later it was changed to Ruckelville. The upper terminal of Ruckel's portage was still known as Cascades, Oregon. Later it was sometimes known as The Falls, Oregon and still later as Portageville, Oregon. When the steamboat locks were built there in the late eighteen hundreds it was changed to Cascade Locks.

In May 1853 only four white adults with two small boys lived at what is now Cascade Locks. Two white adults and two small children lived at what is now Stevenson, Washington. Changes came fast, thousands of emigrants poured across the plains and over the portages with some of them remaining at the Cascades. On the south bank where Cascade Locks is now, a sawmill and steamboat ways were built on the Attwell donation land claim. The sawmill was powered by an overshot water wheel on what is known as Attwell Creek, logs were brought to the mill with ox teams, often six yoke or twelve oxen. With primitive hand tools, working twelve hours a day, these workmen built the steamboat MARY and launched her in September. The following year the Wasco was built at the same place.

1857 the sternwheeler HASSALO was built on these same ways, a 561 ton, 187 feet long steamer ran until 1865.

1860 the sidewheeler IDAHO of 278 tons, 147 feet long was built here.

This was the boat-building capitol of the middle river.

1860 CENSUS (Some Names Misspelled)

FALLS RIVER PRECINCT P.O. CASCADES, OREGON

Leonard	Dan	40	Farmer	N.H.
	Sarah	24		Tenn.
	Francis	2		Oregon
Gage,	Henry	29	Laborer	N.H.
Colville,	Rodger	22	Laborer	Penna.
Nickerson,	John	24	Laborer	N.Y.
Harmon,	William	56	Blacksmith	England
Lacy,	Michael	28	Laborer	Ireland
Chipman,	John	32	Farmer	N.C.
	Amanda	32		Va.

142

Chipman,	Henrietta	8		Oregon
	Van Wasco	6		"
	Walter	2		"
Sherwood,	Fred	28or38	Painter	N.Y.
Snook,	Charles	25	Carpenter	N.Y.
Braden,	William	29	" "	"
Attwell,	Roger	39	Master Carpenter	N.Y.
	Mary	40		Tenn.
	Charles	13		Ill.
	Cassius	8		Oregon
	James	6		"
	John W.	2		"
	Harrison	3/12		"
Jones,	Joseph T.	24	School Teacher	Ohio
Thrastle,	Thosmas	27	Farmer	England
Moon,	James	30	Laborer	S.C.
Choate,	Freeling	28	Farmer	Tenn.
Humphrey,	Henry	36	Laborer	Ohio
	Jane	20		Red River
Burstow,	Mary	12		Oregon
Gurta,	Emma	3		Wash. Terr.
Finley,	Mary	7		" "
Vanderpool,	Marion	30	Farmer	N.C.
	Nancy	22		Iowa
Lewis,	William	4		Oregon
	Matilda	2		Wash. Terr.
Ruckel,	Joseph T.	47	Agt.O.Ng. Co.	N.Y.
Hamilton	??	40	Laborer	R.I.
	Priscilla	26		Mapouce
	Mary	9		" "
Witt,	C.J.	45	Wood cutter	Tenn.
Holman,	Jno	50	Carpenter	N.J.
Sanders,	John	40	Laborer	Ind.
Scott,	Wm.	23	"	N.Y.
Howard,	Francis	27	Saloon Keeper	England
Grover,	Chas.	29	Laborer	Tenn.
Esterhart	Jim	35	Painter	England
Waling	Tos	34	Farmer	Ireland
	Elizabeth	24		"
Cox,	Timothy	30	Laborer	Ireland
Miller,	David	30	"	Scotland
Duffy,	Nath.	30	"	Ireland

Layerys,	H.G.	33	"	N.Y.
Ciman,	J.W.	31	Farmer	Va.
	Rachael	25		Canada
	Ella	7		Calif.
	Victor	2		Oregon
	Walter	5/12		Oregon
Wilson,	Harry	35	Laborer	Ill.
Allen,	Jos. M.	45	Carpenter	Mass.
	Nancy	32		Ill.
	Harriet	10		Iowa
	May A.	9		Oregon
	Elizabeth	2		"
Palmer,	C.J.	26	Farmer	Ky.
Gordin,	Jas.	35	Laborer	Ireland
McAllister,	Clarke	21	"	Iowa
Wells,	Wm.	21	"	Unknown
McMillan	Wm.T.	34	Wood Cutter	N.Y.
Flagg,	Orlando	33	Laborer	Mass.
Grady,	J.N.	38	"	Ireland
Doyle,	Rick	29	"	Ireland
Shea,	John	38	"	"
Daly,	Pat	31	"	"
Tamell,	Mikall	32	"	"
Frazer,	J.W.	32	Civil Engineer	N.Y.
Riley,	Jn.	19	Laborer	Ireland
Lulliman,	Michall	29	"	"
Cummings,	Michall	38	"	"
Foster,	Silas B.	36	"	Vt.
Hansen,	Jn.	24	"	Ireland

(above reside at Eating House)

Part of Letter written by Captain Coe

"The 'HASSALO' was fast completed and then placed in commission. She was a side-wheel boat, some better than the 'MARY' but a poor excuse; not up to date for even then.

"About this time R.R. Thompson, a sheep man and Indian agent living at The Dalles, and L.W. Coe, then manager for the Bradfords, conceived the idea of placing a boat on the upper Columbia. This was considered a very hazardous undertaking as this part of the river was very swift and filled with rapids, but the business outlook was very bright and they decided to take the risk, and a boat about 140 feet long was built at the Cascades and named the 'VENTURE'. She was to be taken to The Dalles and hauled around the falls at Celilo, but never reached her destination. On the day she was to make her trial trip, and while landing above the Cascades on the Washington side, through misunderstanding with the engineer, her lines were cast off before sufficient steam was had to stem the current, and she drifted helplessly over the rapids, escaping destruction only by a miracle. She was afterwards sold and the Col. Wright was built at Celilio the same year, the material being hauled from The Dalles by teams 15 miles to the mouth of the Deschutes."

Colonel Wright

It has not been mentioned in early history why the steamer was named after the Colonel but we will guess that he had a financial interest in the steamboat. He was commanding army troops at The Dalles.

The COLONEL WRIGHT ran up the uncharted upper river until 1865 when she was dismantled. This same year Wright a brigadier general, took an ocean trip with his wife and tragedy struck. He and his wife stood on the deck of the sinking BROTHER JONATHAN in a storm off the California coast. He pleaded with his wife to step into a lifeboat which would take the women and children, while he would stay as a soldier must. She refused to leave his side. A survivor said his last view was of General Wright wrapping his military cloak tenderly around her, and together they stood as the ship went down.

George Iman mentioned, "Isaac H. Bush, early day Pioneer, deserves to be mentioned, a man of much hospitality. It was he who built a hospital near the blockhouse for the benefit of the sick emigrants that crossed the pioneer trail to help build our country."

*Isaac Bush was not the writer the Bradfords were, also there was only one Isaac Bush and several Bradfords. It is noted tht Mr. Bush had the steamer MARY built, on the Attwell boatways where many years later the Wind River Co. sawmill was located at Cascade Locks. Letters show that the steamboat was built for Mr. Bush and a room on the MARY was known as the Bush room. Later the Bradfords took over the steamer and the railroad, how the exchange was made, we do not have details. We do know that bad feelings developed between Mr. Bush and the Bradfords. In the partnership it was several brothers out voting one outside the family. Bradfords gradually took over, it became Bradford's Landing, Bradford's Portage, Bradford's steamboats. The three Bradfords were merchants from Massachusetts and had money to work with. Daniel was the oldest and was 33 years old when filing his donation land claim at the Cascades.

Earl Henry, nephew of Turner Leavens, gives us this story:
"Turner Leavens did not arrive at the Cascades until 1859 and at the early age of 8 years, however, he was a good story teller. His father, Dr. Leavens, arrived in 1852 so no doubt passed these stories on to Turner. One of these stories is:
"Isaac Bush and D.F. Bradford in the early fifties staked out their land claims, so that the claims overlapped, and when the government survey came more troubles commenced and a lawsuit resulted, which was carried through the courts until Bush became short of funds.

146

"There was a man at that time by the name of Edmond Sullivan, a master carpenter, in the employ of the O.S.N. I think he was building the steamer Idaho, at the Upper Cascades, on the Oregon side of the river. (The side-wheeler IDAHO was built at the Attwell boatyard in 1860. 278 tons, 147 feet long.)

"He was a fearless man. I think the first I remember seeing Mr. Sullivan was in the spring of 1860. He came to our house early in the morning before we were up, with a prisoner who had killed a man by the name of Andrews at the Upper Cascades. The prisoner's name was Donovan. Sullivan had volunteered to arrest the man and had walked him from the Upper Cascades to the Lower Cascades, about five miles, and turned him over to my father, who was sheriff at that time; nobody knows the facts about the killing. It was in the night and no one saw it but the two. It was done between Bradford's store and the mainland. The store was built on a little island, with a railroad bridge and also a foot bridge connecting it with the mainland. (This must have been Bradford's warehouse instead of the store.) Donovan claimed that Andrews was about to throw him off the bridge and he shot in self defense. They were both drunk and it was generally believed that it was a friendly bout to start with. They were apparently friends and got drunk together and I think they were both working for Sullivan on the steamer IDAHO on the Oregon side of the river.

"Now this man Bush had quite a large family, four sons, I think, and three daughters. Bush owned a two-story hotel. Some of his sons were at this time grown men. (1860 census shows George W. 23, James J. 19, Cyril F. 17.) All carried guns, everybody did at this time.

"The only gun then was the old Colts muzzel loading revolver. Jay Bush, not the oldest son (could be nickname for J.J. Bush), if he was drinking and if crossed in that mood, was sure to cause trouble and perhaps do some shooting, as shooting was his strong suit. George and Ed Bush were a little cooler and more reasonable and did not take to drink very much. (1960 census shows Cyril as the brother that Turner calls Ed?)

"Ed Sullivan was by this time sheriff of the county. In June 1864 on the Territorial election day, the election was held in the Ferguson Hotel. The election officials were counting the votes in a room next to the saloon when the trouble started. The Bushes had adopted an Indian boy and raised him with the family. He was known as Johnny Bush. He and the three Bush boys and a man known as 'Five-Fingered Baker' were the main plotters.

"Johnny Bush fired the first shot. Sullivan, the sheriff, was in the room where votes were being counted. When he heard the shot he thought sure it was Jay Bush and went directly to meet him. Finding him sober and not excited, he asked him who fired the shot. Jay said he did not know, that it was done outside. Sullivan went outside and met Ed Bush, who was asked the same question. Ed did not answer but drew a knife and struck Sullivan in the side of the neck. Sullivan would have made short work of Ed only George Bush was standing nearby. George pulled his gun and shot Sullivan but did not kill him instantly. Denison, hearing the racket, rushed out just as George was ready to shoot Sullivan the second time. He grappled with George and took his gun and fired it at him, shooting him in the hand. George fell over backwards and went into the river. Being a good swimmer he went on down with the current to his father's home, about 400 feet below. Jay Bush, who had up to this time been standing watching the fight, now seeing George, as he supposed, killed, and Ed badly cut, shot Denison, mortally wounding him, and then turned the gun on Sullivan. By this time Ed Bush was on the run as fast as he was able, which was not very fast. Sullivan was also very weak from loss of blood but he did not pay any attention to Jay Bush's shooting and followed Ed Bush one hundred feet before he fell."

"And here is the strangest part of the whole affair. Sullivan had a good navy revolver in his scabbard on him and well loaded, and why he did not use it, nobody knows. It was supposed that Jay Bush followed Sullivan and Ed until Sullivan was done for and then hurried on to see how badly his brother was hurt. When he got home he found his other brother, George, there, only shot through one hand, otherwise all right. Ed was pretty badly chopped up. Jay supposed until then that his brother George was dead, for he had seen him shot and had seen him fall into the river.

148

"Denison lived until the following day, but expired on the boat before it reached Portland. Each of the men, Sullivan and Denison, left a wife and children. Sullivan had one son and two daughters. Captain Edmond Sullivan, now a first class pilot on the lower Columbia River, is the son of Mrs. Sim Barton of Portland, the oldest daughter. The youngest daughter, I think, lives in Klickitat. Mrs. Sullivan later married J.L. Ferguson, who was later United States inspector of hulls in Portland.

"That was a wild night, there being a large crowd gathered there for election and waiting for the votes to be counted when the shooting started, which I think was intended to frighten the people as all the shooting except what George and Jay Bush did, seemed not aimed at anybody in particular. The crowd scattered in all directions. One lot that belonged at the Lower Cascades lit out without any light of any kind, down the railroad, and when they got about the center of the high trestle they heard a hand car coming. Afraid to make a try to finish crossing the bridge, they dropped through between the ties and hung until the car passed over them. But they misjudged the distance that the car was from them and they had to hang on there so long that some of them were unable to raise themselves again. One, however, was able to get up and by hard work managed to get others up, but one large man by the name of Peter Dulgerson was exhausted and came very near falling to the ground, which would have added one more to the feud, as the bridge was over seventy feet high.

"One man, S.M. Hamilton, who was one of the judges of the election, had a stray bullet pass through his beard that burned his face. For several days after the shooting the Upper Cascades was topsy turby. There were over twenty-six men hunting for the Bush boys everywhere in the woods, but for some reason none of them went to the Bush house and it seems to me they had cold feet. I don't remember that they had any trouble taking them into custody; I think that they gave themselves up peaceably.

"It was established at the trial that 'five-fingered Baker' and the Indian boy, Johnny Bush, did all the shooting, that is, nearly all, but they did not hit anybody. Baker swore in court that he fired twenty-six shots. My memory is that the

149

Bush brothers were all acquitted. I do not know their plea but I think it was self-defense. I did not hear the trial."

* * * * * * * * * * * *

This volume 'One' covers some of the early history around the Cascades from 1805 into 1865.

Volume 'Two' which is now being prepared for the printer will continue this early history into the 1900s.

The author wishes to extend thanks to the ones who have helped him compile this history.

Mrs. D.M. Coon
The Hood River Library Staff
Lottie and Wayne Gurley
The Oregon Historical Society
The Northwest History Section of the Washington
    State Library Staff
Polly Attwell and the Attwell letters

Hamilton and Griswold oxen freight line from the lower steamboat landing on Hamilton Island to Chenwith's mule powered portage railroad around the rapids 1852 until March 26, 1856, when Griswold was shot by the Indians.

Other Books Published

TAHMAHNAW—The Bridge of the Gods
COLUMBIA RIVER GORGE HISTORY *VOLUME TWO*
TAHLKIE BOOKS *(Tahlkie is an Indian word for Yesterday)*